50
OBJECT
LESSONS

50
OBJECT
LESSONS

Donald J. Poganski

THE GOSPEL VISUALIZED
FOR CHILDREN

CONCORDIA
PUBLISHING HOUSE
3558 SOUTH JEFFERSON AVENUE
SAINT LOUIS, MISSOURI 63118

Concordia Publishing House, St. Louis, Missouri

© 1967 Concordia Publishing House

10 11 12 13 14 15 16 17 MAL 91 90 89 88 87

DEDICATION

To Doris
David
Karen
Cynthia

CONTENTS

PREFACE

This volume of object lessons visualizes the good news of Christ's saving love. May it help you declare this central message of the Bible, for "it is the power of God for salvation to everyone who has faith." (Rom. 1:16)

The value of teaching with object lessons is in opening the "eye-gate," and this in turn opens the "ear-gate." Then the truth reaches the home of the heart.

The object lessons presented are time tested, having been used by the author in doctrine classes of children and youth, in Sunday schools, daily vacation Bible schools, and in introductions to sermons. Many of them are original with the author. Some were received in kernel form by word of mouth from pastors and teachers and were developed into the present form. Others were adapted from printed materials by permission of authors and publishers. If there is a resemblance in any other lessons to a printed source, indulgence is asked, for the source was not known to the author.

Many of the lessons in this volume can be used by pastors and teachers in teaching Christian doctrines. The objects should be well prepared, for they will be useful year after year. Many lessons will be helpful for Bible story teaching. The lessons are built around a Bible verse or verses, and in most of the lessons reference is made to one or more related Bible stories.

Bible quotations are from the Revised Standard Version unless otherwise indicated.

A few simple rules apply in teaching with object lessons.

1. Keep the element of surprise in the lessons by building up to the goal step by step.
2. Wherever possible involve the audience by questions and by representative participation.
3. Prepare and practice well beforehand.
4. Never overuse this method. Keep it fresh by occasional use.

Many of the objects used in the lessons are more than attention-getting devices. They serve as continual aids in the presentation of the lesson. Proper attention is given to the relationship of one doctrine to another. Also, emphasis is given to the doctrines of sin and grace so that those who are taught divine truth will encounter Christ as their personal Savior from sin. Christ's saving love alone gives growth and power to manifest faith in daily Christian living.

Appreciation is expressed to the following authors and publishers for permission to adapt materials.

Ferntheil, Carol. *Object Talks with Paper and Scissors.* Cincinnati: The Standard Publishing Company, 1961.

De Golia, J. E. *Object Lessons . . . Using Common Things.* Wheaton: Scripture Press, 1954.

Huxhold, Harry N. *Adventures with God.* St. Louis: Concordia Publishing House, 1966.

Kruse, Wilfred F. "Chemistry Applied to Teaching Religion," *Lutheran Education,* 1954, lxxxix, 7, 317.

Wilder, Elmer L. *Favorite Object Lessons, No. 4.* Grand Rapids: Zondervan Publishing House, 1960.

Wilder, Elmer L. *See It! Object Lessons.* Grand Rapids: Zondervan Publishing House, 1945.

Christ Calls Us to Grow (Sunday School Leader's Guide)
    Minneapolis: Augsburg Publishing House, [1958]

Other fine object lessons which the author has found helpful may be found in the books listed in the bibliography.

It is my prayer that these pages may exalt the Gospel of Christ in the hearts and lives of many so that those who hear and believe become a visual Gospel for the world to read.

1. A VERY SPECIAL GIFT

(God's Christmas Gift to the World)

Materials

A cardboard box (square), cut so that it opens to form a cross. Paint the cross red, and place a picture of Jesus on the center section. On the flaps print the names of some of the blessings Jesus brings: faith, peace, joy, life, love. Wrap the box in plain brown paper, and attach a ribbon. Attach card: To: World, From: God.

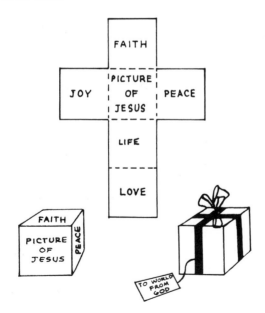

At Christmastime we like to give and receive gifts. There is always much anticipation. We can hardly wait to open the gift package to see what is in it.

I'm holding a very special gift. The card says, "To: World," "From: God." What could the gift be? Let us unwrap it. Just look! It is a picture of Jesus. This gift has a message for us. "God so loved the world that He gave His only Son, that whoever believes in Him should not perish but have eternal life." (John 3:16)

Look at the picture of Jesus. He is so kind. You can almost hear Him say, "Let the little children come to Me." He is so full of love. You can almost hear Him saying: "Your sins are forgiven." When Jesus was born, an angel announced to the world: "For to you is born this day in the city of David a Savior, who is Christ the Lord" (Luke 2:11). One day when Jesus was going about His ministry, He talked to Nicodemus and said: "God so loved the world that He gave His only Son." Jesus is indeed God's Christmas gift to the world.

God gives great blessings with His gift of Jesus. (Unfold the flaps one by one.)

God gives us faith to accept Jesus — "Whoever believes in Him should not perish." Believing is trusting that God takes our sins away because of Jesus.

God gives peace. Peace is the settled attitude of believing hearts that are right with God. The Christmas angels sang, "Glory to God in the highest, and on earth peace among men with whom He is pleased." (Luke 2:14)

God gives joy. Joy is like a "happiness flag" that is flown from the believer's heart when Jesus is in residence there. The Christmas angel announced, "Behold, I bring you good news of a great joy which will come to all the people." (Luke 2:10)

16

God gives life — "Whoever believes in Him . . . [shall] have eternal life."

God gives love. "We love because He first loved us" (1 John 4:19). "Beloved, if God so loved us, we also ought to love one another" (1 John 4:11). At Christmastime people often show their love by giving gifts. At all times we should show our love to God by giving Him our hearts and lives in loving services and then showing love to others.

God's Christmas Gift to the world had such humble wrappings — a manger, a stable, a lowly mother; just as this gift is wrapped in brown paper. This is to teach us that the content of the gift is most important. His Son is true God and able to be the world's Savior. Look at this gift how it unfolds into a cross. Jesus came to shed His holy, precious blood on the cross to pay for the sins of the world. It is most urgent that we and all people have God's Christmas Gift. It makes the difference between eternal death and eternal life — "Whoever believes in Him should not perish but have eternal life."

2. THE BIBLE: LOST AND FOUND

Materials

A Bible and secular items such as a merchandise catalog, a TV guide, some magazines, a comic book, and some sports items. Place these items on top of the Bible before the presentation. Begin talking to the group by taking each item and discussing the time spent on these things.

How much time do you spend on sports, reading magazines and comic books, watching TV, and searching the catalog and shopping? Indeed, we spend much time with these things.

What do I find below all this material? It is a Bible. The Bible is a lost book to many people. Is it a lost book to you?

Long ago the Bible became a lost book. The people just neglected it. Then when Josiah, the godly king, was repairing the house of the Lord, the high priest found the Book of the Law. It was perhaps in some closet in the house of the Lord—even neglected in church! They lost the source of divine power. No wonder the people were not diligent in spiritual things! No wonder they were walking in evil ways! The high priest showed the book to the scribe, and the scribe brought it to Josiah. Josiah had the scribe read it to him. He was very sorrowful because the people had neglected the Word of God. He ordered the Book of the Law read to them; Josiah and the people pledged to follow it.

And the king stood by the pillar and made a covenant before the Lord to walk after the Lord and to keep His commandments and His testimonies and His statutes with all his heart and all his soul, to perform the words of this covenant that were written in this book; and all the people joined in the covenant. (2 Kings 23:3)

A new, more God-pleasing life followed.

The Bible is not a lost book but a *found* book if we read it daily and live according to it.

The Christians at Berea searched the Scriptures diligently (Acts 17:10-11). Lois and Eunice searched the Scriptures and taught young Timothy (2 Tim. 1:5, 3:14-17). The early Christians continued in the teachings of the Scriptures (Acts 2:41-42). Above all, the Bible gives us Jesus Christ.

3. BY CHANCE OR CREATION?

Materials

Ten pennies, numbered 1 through 10

Here are 10 pennies numbered 1 through 10. I now hold them in my hands, and I will shake them together. I will drop them out of my hands one after another. What chance is there that numbers one and two would drop out in order? Perhaps one in a hundred. What chance is there that numbers one, two, and three would drop out in order? Perhaps one in a thousand. Now try to figure out the rest of it! What might the mathematical chances be that they should drop out 1 to 10 in succession? This is just a simple chance-illustration to show how impossible and ridiculous it is to assume that this world and mankind just happened by chance.

Consider the wonders of the universe around you. The billions of stars follow their orbits. The earth is just far enough away from the sun to warm it and yet keep it from burning up. The topsoil is just deep enough to grow plants for food. And the earth keeps spinning at a set speed so that we have day and night. Besides, behold the wonders in nature! Birds migrate, seasons change, and seeds grow.

Consider also the wonders of the human body. Man's brain has a vastly complicated array of circuits and more electronic equivalents than a radio and television network. Man's eye is another wonder. The eye is like a city nestled in the mountains of the skull cavity for protection. It is surrounded by a forest; for the eyebrows, like a thick forest, keep enemies from attacking or injuring the eye. The eye is covered with a very strong membrane, the eyelid, which covers the eye when danger is near. The eyelashes, like eaves on a roof, keep things out. The eye has an automatic washer, the tear duct, with just the right solution so that it kills foreign germs but not its own good germs. Like a street washer, the tear duct washes out the dirt and germs that fall in. The eye is like a big color camera on a swivel; it takes and instantly develops pictures of God's creation. The eye is just one of the wonders of the human body. Did this just happen by chance? Not even a few pennies fall in order by chance!

The Bible says: "For in six days the Lord made heaven and earth, the sea, and all that is in them" (Ex. 20:11). The universe came by creation of Almighty God. He made all things out of nothing by His almighty Word (Gen. 1). When we consider the wonders of our bodies, it should move us to praise our Creator God like the psalmist: "I will praise Thee, for I am fearfully and wonderfully made; marvellous are Thy works, and that my soul knoweth right well." (Ps. 139:14 KJV)

God's Word tells us that the almighty Creator made heaven and earth. Many of the works of God's creation are beyond our understanding, but as Christians we say: "By *faith* we understand that the world was created by the Word of God" (Heb. 11:3). And the work of creation is the first statement of the faith we confess in our services every Sunday.

4. CLAY IN THE POTTER'S HAND

Materials

A lump of silly putty

Many children have silly putty for a play item. It is fun to have because so many things can be done with it. When made into a ball, it bounces. When pulled quickly, it snaps. When pulled gradually, it makes a rope. It can be fashioned into any shape a person wishes. Let us use this putty to remind us of some lessons in the Bible about discipleship.

The Bible says that all people are by nature without God and without hope and purpose. They are like silly putty, which left to itself sprawls out in a shapeless mass. People without God's spiritual life have no purpose because they are a "mass" of spiritual death. Silly putty is the color of clay, which reminds us that all people are earthly in the sense of being spiritually dead—"You are dust, and to dust you shall return." (Gen. 3:19)

However, when I take this putty into my hands and work it, it takes on form. In other words, you might say that it puts "life" into it. My hands will represent the hands of God, who through His Spirit works faith in people's lives and reshapes them in His image. God has a definite purpose for His own redeemed. He makes them vessels to bear His name to others. So I shape the putty into a vessel.

The putty stays in the shape of a vessel only so long

as I keep working at it. Otherwise it falls out of shape. As God's children we are to let God continually work in our lives through His Word and let God have His way with us. We read in Jer. 18:2-6 these thoughts about being clay in the potter's hand: "Go down to the potter's house . . . and he reworked it into another vessel, as it seemed good to the potter to do. Then the word of the Lord came to me: 'O house of Israel, can I not do with you as this potter has done? says the Lord. Behold, like the clay in the potter's hand, so are you in My hand, O house of Israel.' " What God desired to do for Israel, He will do for everyone. We need to respond as Isaiah did, saying: "Yet, O Lord, Thou art our Father; we are the clay, and Thou art our potter; we are all the work of Thy hand." (Is. 64:8)

God does not make His children into balls of self-concern. When this putty is made into a ball and bounced, it bounces all over. It is unpredictable. Disciples who are bound up in self-concern "bounce" with the whims of life. Peter "bounced" with the crowd in the courtyard. All of Christ's disciples argued about greatness and "bounced" at each other (Luke 22:24-28). So they all left Jesus in His hour of suffering. After His death and resurrection Jesus strengthened His disciples in faith. He began molding them again into fit vessels of mercy. He gave them the Holy Spirit at Pentecost to help them tell others of Him. They went forth bearing the Water of life. They were clay in the Potter's hand.

Jesus called His disciples (Mark 3:13-19). They were shaped by Him and made fit to go forth and preach. They remained His vessels by abiding in faith. If a person departs from the working power of the Potter's hand, then the world can "stretch him into a rope," or "snap" him. This is what happened to Judas.

Let us, like the other disciples, yield ourselves to the Potter's hand, saying,

"Mould me and make me after Thy will,
While I am yielded, waiting, and still."

5. THE CALVARY STORY

Materials

A piece of paper, a pair of scissors, and nine straight pins. Display the pieces on a flannel board or any bulletin board. Fold the paper as illustrated, and cut twice. Arrange as illustrated as you tell the story.

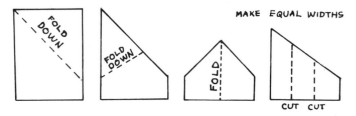

SUPERSCRIPTION

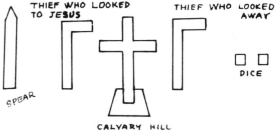

25

The Bible tells us in Luke 23:33-44 that the crucifiers took Jesus to a hill outside Jerusalem called Calvary. They crucified Jesus there. Crucifixion was done by nailing a person's hands and feet to a cross. Sometimes a person was tied to the cross. Jesus was nailed. In order to heap more shame on Jesus, the crucifiers put Jesus between two malefactors or evildoers. One looked away in unbelief; the other later looked to Jesus in faith. The soldiers were only interested in getting the job done and taking Jesus' clothes. They cast lots for His garment. Many people only want some outward connection with Jesus, rejecting His forgiveness. A superscription also was written and placed over Jesus' head. It said: "This is the King of the Jews." Jesus suffered for 6 hours, and then He died. In order to make sure that Jesus really died, a soldier pierced His side with a spear. (John 19:33-34)

Where did the thief go who refused to accept Jesus' forgiveness? (Spell out the letters as follows:

The Bible speaks of hell as a place of torment and remorse. It is where God is not, and there is no light or love, eternally. (See 2 Thess. 1:9, and Matt. 25:46a.) An unbeliever scoffed at a Christian for believing that there was a hell. He said, "You can't even tell where hell is!" The Christian said: "Hell is at the end of a Christless life." He was so right.

Where did the penitent thief go? (Spell out the word life. You will need all the pieces but one.)

LIFE

This thief realized that his earthly life would soon run out. Eternity where? He realized that Jesus would forgive him. He heard Jesus say: "Father, forgive them." He trusted that there was forgiveness for him too. He asked Jesus to remember him when He came into His kingdom. Jesus said: "Today you will be with Me in Paradise." He received the gift of everlasting life. The moment a believer dies, his soul goes to the Paradise of God to enjoy everlasting life. The soul will be united with the body on Judgment Day when it will be resurrected in glory.

Jesus allowed men to nail Him to a cross because He came to be a curse in the place of sinners. "Christ redeemed us from the curse of the Law, having become a curse for us—for it is written, 'Cursed be everyone who hangs on a tree [cross]'" (Gal. 3:13). Not the nails but His boundless love kept Him on the cross. "The Son of man came to seek and to save the lost" (Luke 19:10). "He was wounded for our transgressions, He was bruised for our iniquities." (Is. 53:5a)

6. CANDLES OF CHRIST

Materials

A large white candle, lighted
A small, colored candle, partly burned

Have you ever thought of yourself as a candle? The wax part stands for your physical self. The wick stands for your soul, the realm of thought and feeling. The wick is charred and filthy. By nature you and I are "dead through the trespasses and sins . . . by nature children of wrath, like the rest of mankind" (Eph. 2:1,3). Furthermore, there is no flame. A candle may be very attractive on the outside, but if the wick is not burning, it fails its purpose. By nature you and I are without spiritual light and life, walking in darkness and in the shadow of death (Is. 9:2). Darkness is a symbol of evil and death.

How can we get the flame of the Spirit? How can we glow for God? In Ps. 18:28 we read: "For Thou wilt light my candle; the Lord my God will enlighten my darkness" (KJV). It is God who lights the candles of our lives. God gave His only begotten Son for a light to the world. He is the master candle, as this shining, large white candle. He came to give people the saving light. Light is a symbol of life. He declared: "I am the Light of the world; he who follows Me will not walk in darkness, but will have the light of life" (John 8:12). He died for all the sins of the world in the darkness of Calvary's cross. He brought light through the forgiveness of sins. Christ comes to man with His offer of forgiveness, as I bring this "Christ candle" to the small candle. The wick is now burning with the light of Christ. Whoever believes in Him has this saving light. With His forgiveness comes spiritual life, freedom from eternal death, and enlightenment. These are His gifts of faith to sin-darkened souls.

In the Bible we read about certain blind people, as blind Bartimaeus (Mark 10:46-52). In spite of his physical blindness and darkness, he saw clearly that Jesus was the Son of David, the Holy One of Israel. He had the inner light of faith. By healing him Jesus showed to others around that He is indeed the Light of the world who came to give light to all who sit in the darkness of spiritual death. It's a double blessing to have both spiritual light and physical sight.

In John 9:5 Jesus declared: "As long as I am in the world, I am the Light of the world." Then He healed another blind man. At the close of the chapter He makes it clear that much worse than physical blindness is spiritual blindness. He emphasized that if people realized their spiritual blindness they would receive Him as the Savior from sin. Without the light of salvation in Christ man's guilt remains. Without Christ there is only eternal death. Most important in this life is that we be candles for Christ. Then we have the promise to dwell in His light eternally. (Rev. 21:23-24)

Every blind person to whom Jesus miraculously restored sight became an object lesson of what Jesus wills to do for man in a spiritual way. Jesus wills to restore man's spiritual sight by the enlightenment of faith. Those in whom this happens become candles for Christ. Then every thought and desire of the soul is brought into subjection to Christ's light in order to glow for Him. (Eph. 5:8-9)

29

7. CHRIST FULFILLED THE LAW

Materials

A pair of white canvas gloves with red cuffs

How many fingers do you see on these gloves? Yes, 10 is right, and that is the number of the commandments. "And He declared to you His covenant, which He commanded you to perform, that is, the Ten Commandments; and He wrote them upon two tables of stone." (Deut. 4: 13). These gloves remind me of the Ten Commandments.

These gloves are to be used for doing things. Would I be using them as the manufacturer intended if I put only one finger of each hand partway in them? No! These gloves are intended to be worn on the whole hand.

I am reminded that some people think they have done all they should do when they have outwardly kept one or two of the commandments. They know it's wrong to bow down to an idol, but they don't realize it is just as wrong to worry and distrust God. They know that it is wrong to rob a bank, but they don't realize that it is just as wrong to steal your neighbor's good name by gossip. They know it is wrong to murder, but they fail to realize that it is just as wrong to hate. So three of my fingers are only partly into the gloves' fingers. That is how people keep God's commandments — only in part!

No one can keep the whole Law — in thought, word, and deed — because all people are born with a sinful nature. "All have turned aside, together they have gone wrong; no one does good, not even one" (Rom. 3:12).

Only Christ has perfectly fulfilled the whole Law. In Matt. 5:17 we read: "Think not that I have come to abolish the Law and the Prophets; I have come not to abolish them but to fulfill them." As I place both hands in these gloves, it is an illustration of the way Christ perfectly fitted into keeping and fulfilling God's law for sinners. He was able to keep and fulfill the whole Law; He offered His holy life and died on the cross as payment for all people who could not keep God's holy law.

This explains why the apostle Paul could say, "For Christ is the end of the Law, that everyone who has faith may be justified" (Rom. 10:14). He poured out His precious blood (red cuffs) as payment for all who broke God's law.

Whoever believes in Jesus Christ is freed from the punishment and threats of God's law. Those who are freed are freed to serve God in holiness of life. The Ten Commandments are our guidelines of service. Those who believe should put themselves in God's service as I put my fingers and thumb into the gloves. We can never serve God perfectly in this life, but we should always try harder. In that way we thank Him for giving us His Son Jesus Christ to save us from the eternal punishment of the Law. We strive to do this out of love and gratitude for God; the red cuffs remind us of God's saving love.

Adapted from: *See It! Object Lessons*
Zondervan Publishing House
(used by permission)

8. CHRIST HUMBLED AND EXALTED
(Humiliation and Exaltation of Christ)

Materials

1. A light bulb with ample cord. Use a low wattage bulb so as not to burn the box or cellophane.
2. A white box with a picture of Christ on the front. Make a large door in the back of the box and a small window in the door. Leave window shutter on. Cover door opening with red cellophane.
3. A larger black box with black cross on top, into which the white box can easily be inserted.

RED CELLOPHANE

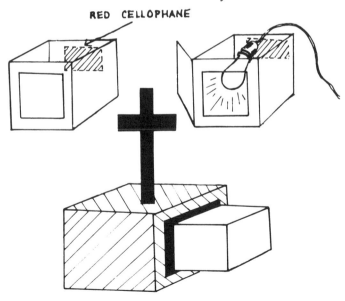

This glowing light reminds us that Christ is the Son of God. From all eternity He shared in the glory and heavenly majesty with the Father and the Holy Spirit. He was true God, Light of light. When man sinned, the Father sent His Son into the world to be man's Savior. So the Son of God chose a human nature of real flesh and was born of the Virgin Mary. I place this light into this white box, which stands for His human nature. The fullness of God entered a human nature! "For in Him the whole fulness of deity dwells bodily" (Col. 2:9 RSV). Christ so humbled Himself in servant form that He did not always and fully use the divine majesty which was given to His human nature. (Phil. 2:5-8)

Once in a while when Christ walked this earth He performed a miracle. For example, He turned water into wine at Cana and His disciples believed on Him (John 2). Every miracle was like opening a window to His divine person. (Open window and have someone look within.) You see a glowing light, don't you? You see it through a red window. This means that Christ performed miracles to prove that He was truly God and able to save people from their sins by the shedding of His blood on the cross. When Christ humbled Himself, He laid aside the use of such attributes as all-knowing, all-present and all-powerful. In inviting men to believe He used them only in part, when it was necessary to prove that He is divine.

Then Christ went to the cross to make Himself a sin offering. (Place the Christ box into the black box, which symbolizes His death and burial.) Christ so humbled Himself that He became obedient unto death, even the death of the cross (Phil. 2:8). He did this to save the sinful, death-deserving world. He was crucified, dead, and buried.

On the third day He rose again from the grave. (Take

the Christ box out and show the reverse side, leaving the window shutter open.) By many signs He showed Himself alive as the true Son of God. He even showed His victory over the devil by His descent into hell prior to coming forth from the grave. He showed Himself for 40 days.

One day He led His disciples to a hill outside Jerusalem. He said, "All power is given unto Me in heaven and in earth . . . lo, I am with you alway even unto the end of the world" (Matt. 28:18-20 KJV). Then He began to rise until a cloud received Him out of their sight. (Open door wide.) He ascended into heaven that He might fill all things. (Eph. 4:10)

This light shines all over. It reminds us of this truth. The light is tinged with red to remind us that Christ is present according to His divine and human natures to carry on His saving work. His presence is one of love and forgiveness which He earned when He humbled Himself and shed His blood on the cross. This illustration cannot convey the deep mystery of Christ's all-presence, for He indeed became invisible. But it does give us an idea of what His presence means for us. He guides people in a gracious way to their heavenly home.

He can be where two or three are gathered together in His name. He can be really present in Holy Communion, as He promised. We are not asked to understand this—just to believe.

He shall come again in full glory on the Last Day to judge the world in righteousness. He will shine in all His glory. (Take red cellophane away). He will then be Judge, for His work as Savior will be ended. Those who accept Him as Savior in their time of grace will enter into His glory. Those who reject Him will be lost forever. (See 1 Thess. 1:7-10; Matt. 25:31-46; and Phil. 2:9-11.)

9. CHRIST STRENGTHENS ME

Materials

A number of short straws.
One nail, the length of the straws.

This straw is a good illustration of a human being. Take this straw in your hand and bend it. It bends easily, doesn't it?Now try to tear it. It tears easily too. A human being is easily bent and torn by the evil world and the devil.

Here is a special straw with a nail in it. The nail stands for the Son of God; He is powerful, because He is God from all eternity. He condescended to come to this earth and become man. He entered human life, just as this nail enters this straw. He came to give divine strength to man.

In Heb. 2:14-15 we read, "Since therefore the children share in flesh and blood, He himself likewise partook of the same nature, that through death He might destroy him who has the power of death, that is, the devil, and deliver all those who through fear of death were subject to lifelong bondage." (See also Gal. 4:4-7.)

As I put the straw with the nail next to the other straw, the straw is supported and strengthened. It cannot be twisted and torn by the world or the devil. This reminds us of living in Christ by faith. The Bible tells us how this takes place. (Quote 2 Peter 1:3-4.)

Joseph was sold by his brothers as a slave. In Egypt, a land of idolatry, he could have gone the ways of the world and lost his faith. But he found strength in his God who promised the Savior. When Potiphar's wife tempted Joseph to commit adultery, he was not bent and broken by the temptation. In his God He had strength. He could say, "How then can I do this great wickedness and sin against God?" (Gen. 39:9)

I think of Moses and Joshua, who were strong in the Lord.

In the Book of Judges we find many strong leaders like Deborah, Gideon, and Samson. Samson for a time thought he had enough strength to fight life's battles alone, but he fell prey to the Philistines. Later he realized that he had to rely on the strength of God alone (Judg. 14—16). (See Heb. 11 for a listing of heroes of faith who found their strength in God alone.)

No life is strong apart from Christ. Some people insist on living their own lives. Others feel that a shallow fellowship with others will help. Still others think that if they keep the right company with decent people their life is safe and meaningful; but they become bent and broken in the end. (Put a straw with a bunch of straws, and show how they all bend.) Only Christ can give the strength that counts and lasts. "I can do all things in Him who strengthens me." (Phil. 4:13 RSV)

10. CHRIST'S REAL PRESENCE IN COMMUNION

Materials

A portrait of Christ by Sallman

One of the most popular portraits of Christ is that painted by Warner Sallman. He painted the portrait after many months of intense study of the life of Christ in the gospels. He saw with the eyes of faith the heaven-drawn picture of the Word of God incarnate. Then with great dedication and personal closeness to Christ he painted the portrait. In it he expressed Christ's tender grace, sympathy, solemnity, truth, kingliness, and love. Around His head is a glow of heaven's light to say: "He is God." The writer to the Hebrew Christians expressed it this way: "God . . . has spoken to us by a Son. . . . He reflects the glory of God and bears the very stamp of His nature, upholding the universe by His word of power. When He had made purification for sins, He sat down at the right hand of the Majesty on high." (Heb. 1:1-3 RSV)

Was it by accident or was it intentional that Sallman painted the light on Christ's face in the form of a wafer and a chalice? It seems intentional. What a grand truth is expressed here! It takes our thoughts to one of the highlights in Christ's earthly life. It was in the Upper Room on Maundy Thursday. He took some of the unleavened bread and wine and after giving thanks gave it to His disciples to eat and drink. He said: "This is My body . . . this is My blood of the covenant which is poured out for many for the forgiveness of sins." (Matt. 26:26-28 RSV)

Christ's real presence in Holy Communion was stated in the Upper Room when Jesus said: "This is. . . ." Wherever this sacrament is administered according to His institution, there He comes with His body and blood as a pledge of salvation. By the Real Presence He enters into the very lives of His own believers to comfort and bless with forgiveness, peace, joy, and strength. Bread and wine are received by communicants in a natural way. His body and blood are received in a way that is supernatural, based on His Word and power to make it true.

The Real Presence in Holy Communion is based on the glory of Christ's person as God. The Real Presence is expressed several times in the Bible, for example: "The cup of blessing which we bless, is it not a participation in the blood of Christ? The bread which we break, is it not a participation in the body of Christ?" (1 Cor. 10:16 RSV). In the same epistle the apostle Paul warns that unworthy communicants, who commune without due thought in a faithless manner, are guilty of profaning the body and blood of the Lord. (1 Cor. 11:27)

The glory of Christ's person invites us to believe that He is truly present in Communion, as He promised. Such a real presence should move those who commune to do so with sincere faith and solemn thought. They are then prepared to receive the greatest pledge of His love that can be received this side of heaven.

11. CHRISTIAN JOY

Materials

A white paper heart (index card weight). A candle. (A strong light bulb in a lamp or extension cord also works and is safer.) Cotton bud and juice of a lemon. Write the word joy on the heart with lemon juice, using the cotton bud. The writing is invisible. When held near the candle flame (or lighted bulb), the writing will become visible.

Believers in Christ receive new hearts through the forgiveness of sins. New hearts are open to spiritual gifts. The spiritual gifts are enjoyed in close fellowship with the Savior. Apart from Him the gifts are not found and enjoyed.

On the afternoon of Jesus' resurrection, two disciples were walking from Jerusalem to Emmaus. While walking they talked about the things that had happened at Jerusalem. Jesus of Nazareth had been crucified. They were very sad. (Luke 24:13-35)

A stranger (Jesus) joined them and talked with them. He showed them from the Old Testament that the promised Christ had to suffer and die and thus enter into His glory. When they arrived at the village, they urged the man to stay with them. They sat down to eat, and when Jesus blessed the bread, they recognized Him. Then He vanished.

The disciples were very close to Jesus. (Hold the heart close to the light.) This light will stand for Jesus, the Light of the world. The heart stands for the disciples' hearts. As they were close to Jesus, they experienced a wonderful spiritual gift. *Joy* came into their lives! Their hearts were warmed by the Word and presence of Jesus. After He left, they said, "Did not our hearts burn within us while He talked to us on the road, while He opened to us the Scriptures?" (Luke 24:32)

As we stay close to Jesus and listen to His Word, we not only find our faith growing and glowing, but the gifts of the Spirit grow too. One of the great spiritual gifts is Christian joy. Joy is the warmth that rises from the fire of faith in believers' hearts when Jesus is present there.

Sometimes disappointments come our way; but when we stay close to Jesus we find that Christian joy carries us through pain.

12. CLEANSED IN CHRIST'S BLOOD

Materials

Six solutions (used in two groups) are needed for this demonstration.

1. Tincture of iodine (2%), vinegar, and cornstarch solution. To prepare the cornstarch solution, use one teaspoon of starch to a pint of water. Make a thin paste and add to boiling water. Then cool. Mix equal parts of vinegar and starch solution. The iodine is to be added during the demonstration.

2. Washing soda: one teaspoonful to a pint of water. Sodium thiosulphate solution (Photographer's "hypo"): four tablespoonsful to a pint of water. Indicator solution (made from one Grove's Bromo Quinine cold tablet). Heat to boiling one-half pint of water and dissolve tablet. Pour off the clear liquid for use in the demonstration. The liquid has a yellowish tinge. Mix equal parts of the three ingredients. Liquid is red. (The phenolphthalein of the cold tablet turns red in the presence of the alkaline washing soda solution.)

To make this demonstration more effective, use two pint jars. One jar for the first ingredients should have an outline of a heart, in white, on the bottom half of the jar. The jar for the second ingredients should have a white cross the size of the jar. Fill the "heart-jar" half full of vinegar and starch solution. The "cross-jar" should be full of the Number 2 solution.

This heart-jar represents the heart of man at Creation. God made man in a special way and made him in His own image. This meant that God put holiness, righteousness, and spiritual knowledge in his soul. As this liquid is white, so the heart and soul of man was sinless.

One day the devil came to man and tempted him to sin (Gen. 3). This bottle of iodine will represent sin. There is a skull-and-crossbones symbol on the bottle as a warning. Iodine taken internally is deadly poison. God told Adam and Eve: "In the day that you eat of it you shall die" (Gen. 2:17). How did Adam and Eve feel toward this command? They disobeyed God and sinned. Sin came into their hearts. As I shake this solution the drops of iodine turn it completely black. Thus sin took control over their whole being. Because of sin, man lost his holiness, righteousness, and spiritual knowledge. Man lost his spiritual life in God and was doomed to eternal death. The Bible says that all people born into this world are sinful (Ps. 51:5) and "the wages of sin is death" (Rom. 6:23). Sin is deadly poison.

Yet God in His great love planned a way for man to be saved. He promised and sent a Savior. (Show the cross-jar full of red liquid.) God sent His Son in the likeness of human flesh, yet without sin. (See Heb. 2:14-15; 7:25-26; and Gal. 4:4-7.) Jesus was truly God-man. He came to do what man could not do. He kept the law of God perfectly for every person and gave His holy life as a sin offering on the cross. He shed His holy, precious blood so that there would be forgiveness for the world of sinners.

Whoever believes in Christ receives personal forgiveness. As the red liquid is poured into the black liquid the heart becomes white and pure again. Thus in God's sight believers in Christ are declared forgiven, free of sin's guilt, and fit for heaven. "The blood of Jesus, His Son cleanses us from all sin. If we say we have no sin, we deceive ourselves, and the truth is not in us. If we confess our sins, He is faithful and just and will forgive our sins and cleanse us from all unrighteousness." (1 John 1:7-9)

Note: The sodium thiosulphate discharges the black color of the starch-iodine solution; the vinegar discharges the red color of the indicator-soda solution. Care should be taken that children do not accidentally taste or swallow the solution. The ingredients can be easily purchased at a grocery store and a drugstore.

In a simple presentation of this lesson use starch solution in a heart-jar and add iodine for sin. Prepare a wooden cross attached to a small jar cover large enough to hold two tablespoonfuls of thiosulphate crystals. Drop it into the black liquid for the cleansing effect.

— Adapted from Wilfred F. Kruse, "Salvation"

Lutheran Education, lxxxix, No. 7, 317 (used by permission)

13. CROWN OF LIFE

Materials

An Eversharp pencil, a ring, and a cross of white cardboard the length of the pencil.

We will let this pencil represent a person as he is by nature. Man by nature is self-sufficient, proud, self-centered. If he makes a mistake, he trys to erase it the best he can. I can think of a man in the Bible who was like that. I think of Saul before he became Paul. He lived for himself and imagined he was right with God. He even thought he did God a service in wronging believers in Christ.

I place this ring on the pencil. This ring stands for the crown of life that Christ earned for everyone. God wants to give it to everyone, for the Lord is "not wishing that any should perish but that all should reach repentance" (2 Peter 3:9). But the ring slips off completely! So Saul could not receive the crown of life, for he proudly served himself. He was yet in unbelief, and "the wicked will not stand in the judgment." (Ps. 1:5)

Now I insert this cross under the clip. I put the crown on again. It stays on because it is held up by the arms of the cross. The cross stands for all that Christ has done for sinners. He died on the cross to take away the sins of the world that sinners might be saved and get to heaven (John 3:16-17). As the cross covers the pencil, so Christ's righteousness covers our sins and makes us right with God.

Saul met Christ on the Damascus Road (Acts 9). He then realized that by himself he would be lost in his sins. By Christ's saving power he received Christ into his heart and life. He knew that the crown of life was his. So he spent his life in Christ's service: telling others how to get right with God and receive a crown of life. Crown is a symbol of honor that believers have in heaven.

We can read about the apostle Paul's joy over the crown of life. He was awaiting death for the cause of Christ. Yet he had courage and great hope. He was right with God. He was sure of the crown of life. He said: "For I am already on the point of being sacrificed; the time of my departure has come. I have fought the good fight, I have finished the race, I have kept the faith. Henceforth there is laid up for me the crown of righteousness which the Lord, the righteous judge, will award to me on that Day, and not only to me but also to all who have loved His appearing." (2 Timothy 4:6-8)

Jesus once said: "Be faithful unto death, and I will give you the crown of life." (Rev. 2:10)

As we look to the Christ of the cross, let our daily confession be:

> False and full of sin I am,
> Thou art full of truth and grace,
> Plenteous grace with Thee is found,
> Grace to cover all my sin.
>
> *The Lutheran Hymnal,* 345

Then when the time comes for God to give the crown, it will be ours. We must be covered with the merits which Jesus earned for us on the cross.

To walk alone is death. To walk with Christ all the way is life.

Which road are you walking?

14. DARK GETHSEMANE

Materials

An 8½×11″ sheet of black paper. A pair of scissors. Fold and cut as illustrated during the presentation.

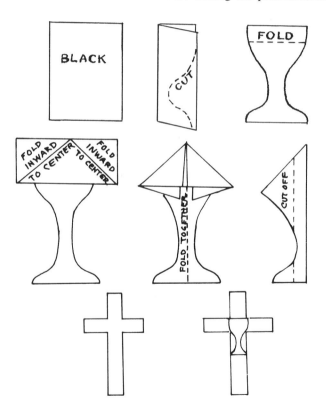

Why was Gethsemane so dark for Jesus? Look at this black sheet of paper. We will let this paper illustrate what made Gethsemane so dark. I fold it and cut out a cup. Jesus said as He prayed in Gethsemane: "Father . . . remove this cup from Me." (Luke 22:42)

What did Jesus mean by the cup? It is picture language for bitter suffering. Surely Jesus knew that Judas would betray Him, that Peter would deny Him, that the disciples would forsake Him, and that the soldiers would nail Him to a cross. All this caused Him suffering. But what did Jesus really mean by His cup?

I will fold this cup and cut it. We see a black cross before us. It is black to remind us that the wages of sin is death. Sin brought eternal death to sinners. Jesus came to take the sinners' place. He would have to taste everyone's eternal death when suffering and dying on the cross. So it wasn't only the physical pain He would have to bear but also the deep sorrow and anguish of His heart and soul when His Father would have to forsake Him while He was on the cross. (See Matt. 27:46.)

When Jesus knelt in Gethsemane, He felt for all sinners the terrible torture of being forsaken by the Father. He could hardly bear to think of it. His sweat became as drops of blood. Jesus prayed for strength to go to the cross and earn salvation for the world.

Since Jesus died for you and me, we have forgiveness of sins. We know God as our Father, and we can always go to Him in Christ's name and ask forgiveness. In Jesus' name we can also talk to our Father in prayer about everything. So:

> "Turn not from His griefs away,
> Learn of Jesus Christ to pray."

In the dark times of our personal "Gethsemanes" we too can talk it over with God. Real prayer is letting God's will shape our will. Jesus not only earned for us the privilege of prayer and empowers our prayers but His prayer becomes a pattern for our prayers. "Father . . . nevertheless not My will but Thine be done." (Luke 22:42)

Note: If you desire to carry the prayer-thought illustration further, see illustration 1a. Begin with a sheet of paper, one side black, the other white. Fold in such a way that the viewers see only the black side. Then when you get to the point of our prayers, you can cut out a cup from the center of the cross. Display the white side, and build your thoughts around Ps. 116:13, "I will lift up the cup of salvation and call on the name of the Lord."

15. DIVINE DIMENSION

Materials

A sheet of white paper. A sheet of brown paper. Make the sheets into cones. Make a "Cross Rho" symbol on the white cone in red letters.

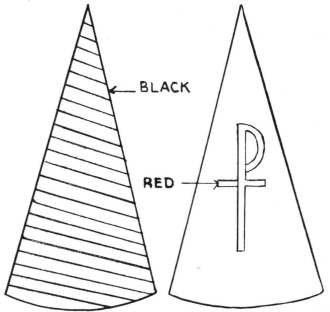

BLACK

RED

Look at this brown cone. It reminds us of human life. The base is broad. Life starts out at the base, and from that moment on it narrows, growing less and less in time. Bodies get older. Soon physical life runs out. Human beings realize this, and it brings a sense of futility. People grasp at temporal straws in an effort to find meaning for life.

But God realized this too. Out of great love for mankind He sent His Son to give man a divine dimension to life.

Look at this white cone. The symbol on it is a symbol of Christ's redemption. The *rho* is the second letter of Christ's name in Greek. The first letter is a *chi* which usually is written as an X. But sometimes the rho is merely crossed with a line to make a cross. The crossline on the rho makes a *chi*. This tells us that Christ died for the sins of the world to bring eternal life to man. He is indeed the One set aside from eternity to be the world's Savior.

I place this Christ cone (inverted) alongside the human cone. It stands for the rebirth that comes through faith. See what a difference it makes to have Christ come into a person's life! It brings a divine dimension to life. And when our earthly life runs out, it is no loss because we shall then receive eternal life in Christ. This is the Christian hope. It puts purpose into living and takes the sting and fear out of dying because the new life in Christ never ends. It is eternal.

The apostle Paul said: "For to me to live is Christ and to die is gain" (Phil. 1:21 RSV). He also said: "I have been crucified with Christ; it is no longer I who live but Christ who lives in me; and the life I now live in the flesh I live by faith in the Son of God, who loved me and gave Himself for me" (Gal. 2:20 RSV). I also think of Simeon, who received the divine dimension and in his old age could joyfully say when he saw the Christ: "Lord, now lettest Thou Thy servant depart in peace" (Luke 2:29). I also think of Anna, quite old but full of hope. (Luke 2:38)

16. FILLED WITH THE SPIRIT

(What Pentecost Means)

Materials

A large, durable, round, red balloon.
A ball-point pen.

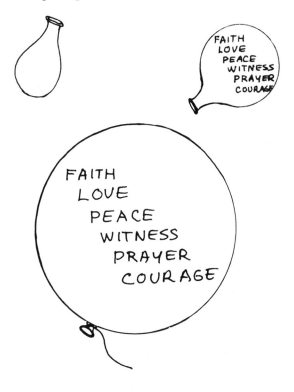

This uninflated balloon will represent all of us as we are by nature. A balloon is made to be inflated with air. Just as this balloon is uninflated and purposeless, so all people by nature lack the Spirit of God.

This balloon is red. The Bible tells us that Christ redeemed the whole world by His precious blood and His innocent suffering and death.

My breath will represent the Spirit of God. In the Bible the Spirit of God is often called the Breath of God. (Inflate the balloon just a little.) See, when my breath enters this balloon, it takes shape, and begins to fulfill its purpose. Let us notice that this balloon did nothing of itself to receive my breath. So man by nature can do nothing to come to faith in Christ. The Spirit of God alone calls man by the Gospel and brings him to faith. Man must receive spiritual life to be saved. The Bible says: "Anyone who does not have the Spirit of Christ does not belong to Him." (Rom. 8:9)

When the Spirit of God enters our lives, He brings us new life and many spiritual gifts. The first gift the Spirit brings is *faith*. I write it on the balloon (write small). (Have the pupils mention other gifts.) The gifts should be: *faith, love, joy, witness, prayer, courage.* Now watch these words as I blow up the balloon to proper size. They get so much larger.

This is what the first Pentecost meant. On that 50th day after Easter the Spirit of God was poured out upon the disciples in full measure so that they were filled with the Holy Spirit. The spiritual gifts that had been begun in them took on greater proportion, and they now began to fulfill their purpose in a life of witness (Acts 2). They told others of Jesus.

The disciples had the Holy Spirit before Pentecost. The fact that they believed in Christ was evidence that "no one can say 'Jesus is the Lord' except by the Holy Spirit" (1 Cor. 12:3). Yet they did not have the fulness of the Spirit. They were so afraid. They lacked courage. They argued among themselves and were sometimes so unhappy. They did not witness boldly. In fact Peter denied Christ just a few weeks before—when one person asked him if he were Christ's follower. When the Spirit of God filled the disciples, the spiritual gifts were enlarged in their lives, and they witnessed courageously. Peter preached to thousands. All the disciples witnessed and went everywhere preaching the Gospel.

Pentecost is not the first time the Spirit of God was active in the world. The Spirit of God was active at creation. He was active in the hearts of Old Testament believers. He inspired the prophets, apostles, and evangelists to write the Bible. He was busy calling men to faith, and He will continue to perform the divine work of bringing men to faith and filling them for service. "They were all filled with the Holy Spirit and began to speak in other tongues, as the Spirit gave them utterance" (Acts 2:4). This is the secret and meaning of the first Pentecost. The rushing wind and divided tongues of fire were only outward symbols of the inner workings of the Spirit.

New Testament Christians can have "Pentecost" every day. The Spirit of God comes to believers as they meditate on God's Word and search the Scriptures prayerfully. That is the pathway to Pentecostal power. God wants us to be Spirit-filled Christians so that we will fulfill our calling to live our whole life for God.

17. FROM FAILURE TO FAITH

Materials

A large capital F with a hook on the top part of the top bar. Make the F double. There should be no hooks on the lower bar. Color the outside of the F black. Leave the inside of the top bar white. Color the part below the top bar red. The top bar is to be cut off to make a capital I and the remaining part becomes a cross.

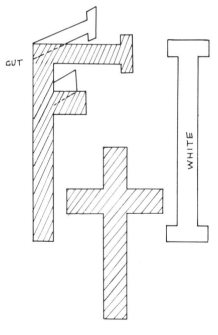

What do you think this letter F stands for? I will give you a hint. It stands for something sin brings to human lives. Yes, it is fear. It is also failure. In John 3, we read of a man named Nicodemus. He was a Pharisee and a ruler of the Jews. He tried hard to live right and be right with God, but his conscience always accused him that he still had not done enough. Without the forgiveness of sins he was fearful and felt he was a miserable failure. Nicodemus even found it hard to sleep nights. Finally he decided to go to Jesus. He was not going to have another sleepless, fearful night.

Jesus recognized Nicodemus' problem immediately. He told him: "That which is born of the flesh is flesh." Jesus added: "Unless one is born anew, he cannot see the kingdom of God." The person who fails to be born anew remains the greatest possible failure.

So Jesus did some spiritual surgery on Nicodemus' heart that night. Just as these scissors cut this letter F to make an I, so Jesus cut into the inner self of Nicodemus to show him his problem. Nicodemus was really in love with himself. He, like other Pharisees, felt he was good enough before God by his good works. But Jesus had Nicodemus take a good look at himself. This letter I is black to remind us of sin. Nicodemus had to see himself a sinner—flesh born of flesh and minus the Spirit. He needed to admit: "I have sinned; I need Christ's forgiveness."

Jesus reminded Nicodemus of an Old Testament story. It was about Moses lifting up the serpent in the wilderness. Jesus said: "So must the Son of Man be lifted up, that whoever believes in Him may have eternal life" (John 3:14-15). (Now show the red side of the remaining part of the F. It's a reminder of the sweet Gospel that Jesus told him in John 3:16.)

When a person comes to the cross, Christ performs the miracle of new birth. The guilt of sin is cleansed, and spiritual life is given. (Show white side of letter I.) That is how Nicodemus looked to God when he received Christ. From John 7:50 and 19:39 it is evident that Nicodemus was a born-again believer. He showed love for Jesus, which is a fruit of faith.

Nicodemus, like other Pharisees, had rejected the Baptism of John the Baptizer and thus rejected the Christ who comes in Baptism. That is why Jesus also said to Nicodemus: "Except a man is born of water and of the Spirit, he cannot enter into the kingdom of God."

When "self" is brought to the foot of the cross with the realization of the need for forgiveness and life, then in Spirit-worked faith Christ is recognized as personal Savior. That's the only way to get rid of the fear and failure of sin.

— Adapted from *Favorite Object Lessons*
Zondervan Publishing House (used by permission)

18. FRUITFUL HEARING OF GOD'S WORD

Materials

A white heart folded as illustrated, with the words *ear, hear, heart*. Outline an ear. Make the T red.

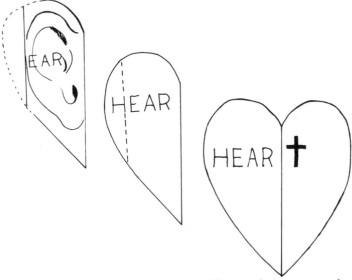

Here is a drawing of an ear. The ear has more to it than is visible on the outside. The inner ear is a very delicate mechanism created by Almighty God, and it makes hearing possible.

So what are ears for? (Turn over the fold H.) Ears are for hearing. This reminds me of something Jesus said once: "He who has ears to hear, let him hear." (Luke 8:8)

He was telling them a story about a sower who sowed seed. Some fell on the road and was quickly eaten by the birds. Some fell on thin soil over rock. The little plants soon withered. Some fell among thorns, and the young plants were choked. But some fell on good ground and brought forth fruit with patience.

In a spiritual way, there is more to hearing God's word than just hearing it with the ear. There must be a hearing with the "inner ear of the heart." (Fold out the T.) The heart is the field where the seed of God's Word is sown.

Notice that this letter T is the shape of the cross. It is red. It stands for God's salvation in Christ's death on the cross. When a heart receives Christ, it becomes fruitful because He brings forgiveness and new life. "So faith comes from what is heard, and what is heard comes by the preaching of Christ" (Rom. 10:17). The heart of every person by nature is poor ground. The ground of the heart must be prepared by the Spirit of God through the Word. The Word is both Law and Gospel. The Law softens the heart by its threats of punishment. In sorrow the heart cries out for mercy. The Gospel is the good news of forgiveness through Christ. This is the seed which enters with new life. The heart that trusts and relies on Christ is honest and good.

Some people hear only with the outer ear. They forget so soon. The devil snatches the Word before it gets to the inner ear of the heart. Some hear with joy at first, but when trials come their way they fall away. Some let worldly cares choke the work of the Spirit. But there are some who receive the word in an honest and good heart.

Jesus made it clear that unless He is received as Savior, the hearing is all in vain. "Secrets of the kingdom" in this parable (Luke 8:10) means the grace of God in Christ. Those who rejected Him as Savior had hearts like roadways, rock, and weedbeds. They could bring forth no fruit to everlasting life.

When Jesus walked this earth in person, He was sowing the Gospel seed. Many turned a deaf ear to Him. But some seed fell on honest and good hearts.

There were some shepherds who listened and found faith.

There were some fishermen who dropped everything to follow Him.

There was a Mary who sat at Jesus' feet and lived for the one thing needful.

There was a Paul who confessed, "I heard a voice," and he gave his life in fruitful living to that Voice.

Now it's our turn. Are you a fruitful hearer of God's Word? Do you make that double confession: I am a sinner; Christ is my Savior? Now look to Gal. 5:22-23 for a heart in full bloom with the fruits of the Spirit.

> Long I wondered at the Sower,
> At His hope for some small gain.
> When the wayside, rocks, and thistles
> Made His labor seem in vain.
>
> But the Sower kept on sowing,
> And His smiling face foretold
> That He found a ground which promised
> Fruit no less than hundredfold.
>
> And the good ground helped the Sower
> To forget the stress and strife.
> For it brought fruit to perfection,
> Fruit unto eternal life.
>
> —W. M. CZAMANSKE

19. GENUINE FAITH OR RELIGIOUS FAKES?

Materials

Some fake candy and chocolate chips.

Give some fake candy to a few of the children. (It looks and smells like candy, but the children will be surprised that they cannot eat it. It is rubber.) Then explain that this candy surely is different in the inside than it appears on the outside. It is fake candy.

There are religious people like that too. This candy reminds me of Cain. He tried to act holy by bringing an offering to God. But his heart was not in it. God was displeased with his offering. God could see that his heart was not right, and so his offering was not pleasing to God. Cain only went through the motions of religion; he really didn't care about God's ways.

Abel was a genuine believer. He brought a lamb as an offering, and God accepted the offering. Already then the lamb offering pictured the great Lamb of God who by the shedding of His blood would take away the sin of the world (John 1:29). Since Abel was genuine in his faith, he did what God prescribed. Genuine faith shows itself in humble acts. Jesus once said that faith, though it be small as a mustard seed, can move mountains. (Give all the children a chocolate chip.) Isn't it sweet and good? The chocolate chip is small but it is genuine. That is what counts. Humble, trusting faith that is real makes people Christians. True faith shows itself in taking God at His word and following His Word about matters of salvation.

We can read this account of Cain and Abel in Gen. 4:1-8.

God's Word says: "Believe in the Lord Jesus, and you will be saved" (Acts 16:31). When faith is genuine, it shows itself in deeds of love. "How much more shall the blood of Christ, who through the eternal Spirit offered Himself without blemish to God, purify your conscience from dead works to serve the living God?" (Heb. 9:14)

Jesus warned the Pharisees about being religious fakes. See the story of the Pharisee and the publican (Luke 18:9-14). The publican who asked for forgiveness was a genuine believer. He was like the chocolate chip. He was small in his own sight but genuine in faith in the eyes of God. He went home right with God.

(Ananias and Sapphira also were religious fakes. You can read about them in Acts 5:1-11.)

20. GOD CARES FOR YOU

Materials

A bowl of water darkened with black ink. A glass. A piece of paper with a red cross and a child's name written on it. Fold the paper and insert in the bottom of the glass so it stays in place when the glass is turned upside down and placed into the water.

As Christians we are in the world but not of the world. The evil of the world around us is very dangerous. The evil world and the devil are constantly trying to get us to fall away. (Display bowl of dark water.) Sometimes things happen to us that seem so troublesome. But we need never lose courage. God cares for His children.

As I put this glass deep into the water, notice that the paper is not harmed. The air in the glass keeps the water out and the paper is dry and protected.

God knows His children by name. "Fear not, for I have redeemed you, I have called you by name, you are Mine" (Is. 43:1). God protects His children because they are worth so much to Him. See the sign of the cross. This reminds us that everyone who believes in Jesus is precious to God because of the worth of Jesus' blood.

God once preserved and protected Noah and his family from the evil world. A terrible flood came to destroy all the ungodly people. But God protected His own who trusted His grace. (Gen. 6 – 8)

God protected Lot (Gen. 19). He protected Daniel (Dan. 6). God protected His own Son (Matt. 2:12-15). As

God protected His own Son in whom the plan of redemption was carried out, so He protects His own who have faith in His Son.

21. HIS WORKMANSHIP

Materials

A wristwatch.

I have been wearing my watch for many years. I don't wear it just because it looks nice. Sometimes it binds my wrist and annoys me. Yet it serves me by telling time, so I wear it.

Let us look at the watch a little closer. It consists of a case, hands, and numbers. If we look inside the case, we see many little gears, all working together to keep time.

This watch just didn't happen by itself. Someone made it. A watchmaker fashioned many parts and put them together so perfectly that it runs and tells time. This reminds me of a Bible verse: "For we are His workmanship, created in Christ Jesus for good works, which God prepared beforehand, that we should walk in them." (Eph. 2:10)

Just as a watchmaker made this watch, so God made us in Christ. God gave us body and soul. Originally, before the fall of our first parents into sin, the soul was righteous and holy. But now every soul is full of sin and doomed to death. "Dead through trespasses and sins" is how the apostle Paul describes it (Eph. 2:1). He goes on to say, "But God, who is rich in mercy, out of great love with which He loved us, even when we were dead through our trespasses, made us alive together with Christ, (by grace you have been saved)" (Eph. 2:4-5).

Whoever believes in Christ is a new creation of God. God's Spirit gives believers a new spiritual life. He gives new desires and goals. God's Spirit "winds the watch" of the new spiritual self which He creates, and puts us, as it were, on the "wrist of God" to serve Him.

This watch is made to run. It is not an ornament. God gives us faith for service. My watch needs hands as well as running parts. If the watch is running and has no hands to tell time, it is useless. Just to hear it tick away would be most annoying. Faith without good works is displeasing to God. Jesus once said: "Not every one who says to Me, 'Lord, Lord,' shall enter the kingdom of heaven, but he who does the will of My Father who is in heaven" (Matt. 7:21). Genuine faith expresses itself in deeds of service. Good works are not necessary for salvation. Christ has done all that is necessary for us to be saved. But once saved, good works are indeed a fruit of faith.

We haven't the ability to serve God perfectly. A watch is not 100 percent perfect in keeping time. The mark of a believer is one of striving for perfection. Striving is the outcome of God's rich grace. Just because He richly forgives our sins and failures every day and never holds them against us, we are so energized by His love that we ask God to "set us the best we can be set" and to empower us to run out our lives for Him.

Why we serve God is summarized in a familiar verse:

> I will not work my soul to save,
> That work my Savior's done.
> But I will work like any slave
> For love of God's dear Son.

When I learn the message of the watch, I am reminded of a Bible story in 1 Samuel 2:12—3:21. Eli was like a slow watch — slow in disciplining his sons and in standing for true morality. Eli's sons were like a stopped watch, for though they were ornaments in priestly service, their lives were not in the service of God. In fact they let the devil use their lives in his service. But Samuel was a workmanship of God's love. "Speak, Lord, for Thy servant hears" was his response of faith. He was faithful in doing God's service and did it with all the might of his hands.

22. THE HOLY CHRISTIAN CHURCH

Materials

A string of imitation pearls. An oyster shell. (If oyster shell is not available, use a box on which an oyster shell is outlined.) Place pearls in shell or box before presentation.

What jewel do you expect to find in an oyster? Naturally a pearl. God has given the oyster the gift to transform a grain of sand into a precious pearl. That reminds us of the transforming power of God's Holy Spirit, who transforms sinful, death-deserving people into children of God and heirs of eternal life.

Within this oyster shell (or box) there is a whole string of pearls. Do you believe that? Take me at my word. All believers are joined together by one faith in one Savior by the spiritual cord of the Holy Spirit. They are the holy Christian church. Since faith is such an invisible gift in believer's hearts, known only by God and the believers, we say: "I believe in the holy Christian church." In heaven we shall see the whole Christian church like a string of precious pearls. Now we open the shell and take a look. The string of pearls is there just as I said. God tells us in His Word that He has to the end of time, and to all eternity, a church of holy believers, made holy by faith in Jesus Christ. The essence of the church is believing people transformed from the loathsome filth of sin into spotless purity by the loving and redeeming Lord Jesus.

Where does one expect to find pearls? Right you are — in an oyster! Where do you expect to find believers? Where the Gospel of Christ is preached. When the Gospel is proclaimed, believers are made. We have God's Word for that. Just as rain and snow water the earth and make it productive, God says, "so shall My Word be that goes forth from My mouth; it shall not return to Me empty, but it shall accomplish that which I purpose, and prosper in the thing for which I sent it." (Is. 55:10-11)

An oyster shell is not very pretty on the outside. It is full of bumps and ridges. Outwardly the church is divided by the ridges of various denominations (name some) and differences in teachings in some doctrines (mention a few). It also has different practices. The church on earth consists of people who still have the old nature of sin clinging to them. Thus there is imperfection in life. Sometimes rather ugly spots may be seen on the church. But we should not gaze upon and magnify them but rather rejoice in its inner glory.

The beauty of the church is seen with the eyes of faith — "I believe!" I am part of that holy church by sincere faith in Jesus Christ. I am one of God's precious pearls. Luther stated it this way: "I believe that there is upon earth a little holy group and congregation of pure saints, under one head, even Christ, called together by the Holy Ghost in one faith, one mind and understanding, with manifold gifts, yet agreeing in love, without sects or schisms. I am also a part and member of the same, a sharer and joint owner of all the goods it possesses, brought to it and incorporated into it by the Holy Ghost by having heard and continuing to hear the Word of God, which is the beginning of entering it."

"As in one body we have many members . . . so we, though many, are one body in Christ" (Rom. 12:4-5).

"Christ loved the church and gave Himself up for her, that He might sanctify her, having cleansed her by the washing of water with the Word, that He might present the church to Himself in splendor" (Eph. 5:25-27). Indeed, the holy Christian church is like a glorious string of pearls.

23. HOW DO WE SIN?

(Sins of Commission and Omission)

Materials

A black heart punched or cut full of holes. A white heart with a red cross in the center. Scotch tape.

Look at this terrible looking heart! It teaches us something about man's sins. The natural heart is active in the service of sin. James says in his epistle: "Then desire, when it has conceived, gives birth to sin" (James 1:15). When a sin is committed in act, this is called a sin of commission. There is also another kind of sin. It is to omit to do what God wills. So this black heart is full of holes. The natural heart cannot do the will of God. James speaks of this, too: "Whoever knows what is right to do and fails to do it, for him it is sin" (James 4:17). This is called a sin of omission.

God in His mercy paid the great price of sending His Son to shed His blood on the cross for the sins of the world. (Show white heart.) One who believes in Christ is forgiven, just as this heart is white in God's sight. In fact believers live by faith in the Son of God. The red cross drawn on this heart reminds us of that. The Bible says: "A new heart I will give you, and a new spirit will I put within you" (Ezek. 36:26). I attach the new heart to the old one.

Notice that the old nature of sin still clings to believers. (Hinge the black heart to the new heart.) Believers are commanded in the Bible to adorn the doctrine of God by a godly life (Titus 2:10). That is, we are to live open lives in Christ, striving to do the things He commands. A list of these things is found in Gal. 5:22-24, and Rom. 12:6-21. If we let this old heart flap over the new one, we surely shut out the life in Christ. That is why James wrote as he did. He warned Christians not to let the old heart flap over. He urged them rather to live for Christ the life that is true. We live for Christ when we realize that sin displeases God, and we accept His forgiveness continually through faith in Christ. We live for Christ when we turn away from sin by the power of His grace, and fight the very sins we confess, always striving to do the things He asks.

To omit to pray or to worship or to be kind and, above all, to omit to speak of Christ to others are sins of omission. To use God's name in vain, to worship one's own ambitions, to be hateful, and to slander others are sins of commission. Let us put these behind us as we fold this natural heart behind, and let us show forth Christ in our daily life.

When Jesus comes in glory, He will renew us completely so we won't have sin anymore—just as I tear off this old nature and cast it aside.

> Before the dawning day
> Let sin's dark deeds be gone,
> The old man all be put away,
> The new man all put on.

24. HOW TO GET TO HEAVEN

Materials

A 5″×7½″ piece of white paper. Fold as illustrated to make an airplane. Cut to make a cross and refold to make a letter T and a letter L.

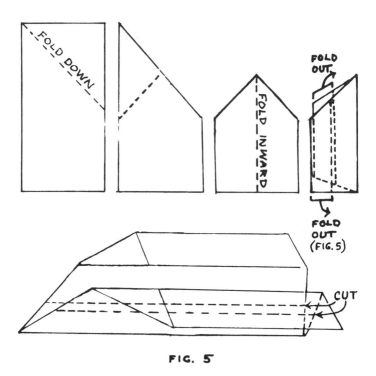

FIG. 5

This little piece of paper will teach us an important lesson. I fold it to make an airplane. This one looks much like a supersonic jet. It is so streamlined. Let's try to fly it. It really goes around the room, doesn't it? Supersonic jets fly at a fast rate of speed. Men have put forth their best work and efforts to make such planes. But did you notice that this paper airplane soon fell to the floor? One thing is sure. You can't get to heaven on a paper airplane or even a supersonic jet. It sounds absurd to even mention it. Yet some people think that they can get to heaven by their own good works. But that is just as absurd as trying to fly in this paper airplane, isn't it?

Some people tried this way to heaven. In Jesus' day there were self-righteous Pharisees (Luke 18:9-12), who did many good works—according to their own ideas. Jesus said of them: "Woe unto you, scribes and Pharisees, hypocrites! for you tithe mint and dill and cummin and have neglected the weightier matters of the Law, justice and mercy and faith; these you ought to have done, without neglecting the others" (Matt. 23:23). All the boasts of the Pharisees of having done enough to be saved were undermined by Jesus' explanation. Their "paper airplane" came crashing down. The Bible insists: "For all who rely on works of the Law are under a curse; for it is written, Cursed be every one who does not abide by all things written in the book of the Law and do them. Now it is evident that no man is justified before God by the Law; for 'He who through faith is righteous shall live.' " (Gal. 3:10-11)

How can a person get to heaven? I will cut the wings off this paper airplane. See, it unfolds to make a cross. There is one sure way to heaven. It says in Gal. 3:13: "Christ redeemed us from the curse of the Law, having become a curse for us—for it is written, 'cursed be everyone who hangs on a tree.'" Christ was nailed to the tree of the cross. He gave His holy life as a payment for all our offenses against God's holy law.

The cross is the only way to heaven. The cross says: "Christ paid for our sins." There should be no doubt about it. Jesus seals that "cross way" to heaven with the word truth. "I am the Truth," He said. This T stands for truth. Jesus does not lie. The Bible does not lie (John 17:17). Let us take Jesus at His word that the merits He earned for us on the cross are sufficient to save us and get us to heaven. Jesus also added, "I am the Life." This L stands for life. Jesus now gives new spiritual life to believers by faith, and this life has no end. It will continue everlastingly. That's heaven.

There is only one way to heaven—the way of Christ's cross.

25. IMAGE OF GOD

Materials

A pint jar. (Paste an outline of a heart in white on the outside.) A white piece of paper to fill the inside. A black strip of paper the same size as the white. A symbol of the Holy Spirit (dove) in white, the size of the heart.

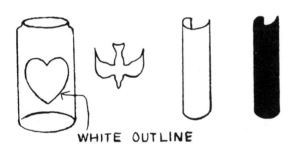

WHITE OUTLINE

God said: "Let Us make man in Our image, after Our likeness. . . . So God created man in His own image, in the image of God created He him" (Gen. 1:26-27). "Then the Lord God formed man of dust from the ground and breathed into his nostrils the breath of life; and man became a living being." (Gen. 2:7 RSV)

What is meant by the image of God? What is meant by "a living being," or as the KJV says, "living soul"?

Let us think of it like this. Here is a clear jar on which there is an outline of a heart. This heart will remind us that God made man and gave him something special — a soul. The breath of life came from the living God. Man was made to live in and with God eternally. Thus man has a property which is God's, namely, continued being, or existence.

On man's soul God placed some special graces. These graces consist of righteousness, holiness, and spiritual knowledge. This piece of white paper is now placed in the jar. It reminds us of the graces which God put upon man's soul at creation. We know from other parts of the Bible that righteousness, holiness, and spiritual knowledge make up the image of God. The apostle Paul wrote to believers at Ephesus that they were to "put on the new nature, created after the likeness of God in true righteousness and holiness" (Eph. 4:24). He also wrote to believers at Colossae and reminded them of the blessings that were theirs since they had "put on the new nature, which is being renewed in knowledge after the image of its Creator." (Col. 3:10)

Man was so created in the image of God that he could live in God and be very happy forever. Man could freely serve God and enjoy praising Him.

But then came the fall into sin. What happened when Adam and Eve sinned? As I remove this white piece of paper, we are reminded that they lost the image of God. Now I insert a black strip of paper and we are reminded that sin and death filled their souls. The soul of man became like a coffin full of eternal death. Mankind by nature lacks true righteousness, holiness, and spiritual knowledge. "Death spread to all men because all men sinned" (Romans 5:12). The Bible emphatically tells us that the offspring of Adam and Eve were born without the image of God. "[Adam] became the father of a son in his own likeness, after his image" (Gen. 5:3). Because man is without the image of God, eternal death is his destiny unless something happens to change it.

Something did happen! God in His great love planned a way for man to receive the image again. He sent His Son to pay the penalty of man's guilt and to die his death. Whoever believes in Christ as Savior, receives His Spirit. "Because you are sons, God has sent the Spirit of His Son into our hearts" (Gal. 4:6). "You are not in the flesh, you are in the Spirit, if the Spirit of God really dwells in you" (Rom. 8:9). I place the Holy Spirit symbol in front of the black paper. Now we have an idea what it means for the believer to have the image of God partially restored in the new birth of faith. It is the spiritual image of faith by the Spirit. Much of the heart is still black, for sin is still present in the form of the old nature. Sin, however, is not at the controls of the heart and life but the Spirit. By the Spirit we already enjoy the image of God, in that we have Christ's righteousness and holiness by faith.

As long as the Spirit of Christ is in the believer's heart, he is a child of God and an heir of heaven. And in the believer's life there is a warfare against sin and evil until he goes to heaven.

Then, upon receiving the full glory of the resurrection body at Christ's second coming, he shall be free from sin's presence forever. I remove the black piece of paper and insert the white one again. The old nature of sin remains in the grave, gone forever. In heaven the full image of God will be restored to them that are in Christ Jesus. The psalmist David expressed it this way, "I shall behold Thy face in righteousness; when I awake, I shall be satisfied with beholding Thy form." (Psalm 17:15)

26. INVESTMENT FOR ETERNITY

Materials

A box labeled, "God's Bank," with a long slit on top and a bottom that opens. (Gold-colored box is preferable to plain.)

Cards: (size that inserts in the slit).

On card 1 print *GRACE*, on reverse side *FAITH*.

On card 2 print *TIME*, on reverse side *70 YEARS, 525,600 MINUTES A YEAR*.

On card 3 print *TREASURES*, on the reverse side *$325,000.00*.

On card 4 print *TALENTS*, on reverse side, *SPEAK-ING, SINGING, TEACHING*, etc., and a question mark.

GRACE	TREASURES

TIME	TALENTS

Did you know that you are God's bank in which He keeps the valuable things of life? What does God keep in His bank?

First there is *grace*. God has a special kind of love which He invested in our lives. He favors us with forgiveness of sins which Christ won for us. (Deposit *grace* into the bank.)

Second, there is *time*. God gives us a period for living on earth. (Deposit *time* in the bank.)

Third, there are *treasures*. God gives each of us what we need in the form of *money* to purchase things for life. (Deposit treasures in the bank.)

Fourth, there are *talents*. Talents are special gifts for doing things. (Deposit *talents* in the bank.)

When banks are open, the savings are used. You are God's bank, and you too are to be "opened." God's bank has a special opening. The bottom opens wide. Here are God's investments in you. (Show reverse side of the cards.)

Grace means faith for you. Grace brings faith. You can live in daily trust in God as your Father. You trust Him to lead you in His way. You can live unafraid. This faith you can share with others when you tell them of God's grace. (Give *grace* card to someone.)

Time means many minutes—over 525,000 each year. The Bible says that the average life is 70 years long. Time is an opportunity to be born again, to worship and serve God. You serve God when you take the time to tell others of Him and to worship with others. (Give *time* card to someone.)

Treasures are the many dollars we earn in a lifetime. When we give our firstfruits to God for church work, like missions and support of charity, we are investing our money in a God-pleasing way. (Give *treasures* card to someone.)

Talents are the many things we can do, like speaking to others of Jesus, teaching, singing. The question mark is for what your occupation will be in life, or what it is. When we use our talents, we are helping others along the way of eternal life. (Give *talents* card to someone.)

Let us study God's banking method as found in Luke 16:1-13. A certain man was a steward, or manager, for a rich man. He misapplied the funds entrusted to him. The master found out that he had taken money and goods for his own pleasures. The rich man told him he would lose his job.

The man was troubled. He wondered what he would do for a living in the future. And he thought: "I will use my last few days in this job to take care of my future. I will call the people who owe my master and bargain with them." The steward then deducted from the bills of the various creditors to make them his friends (vv. 5-7). When the rich man heard of the steward's business procedure, he couldn't help but commend him for his foresight.

Jesus said that many worldly business people are wiser than the children of light, the Christians. Then He made the point clear to them. He said: "Make friends for yourselves by means of unrighteous mammon [money], so that when it fails they may receive you into the eternal habitations." (V. 9 RSV)

In His banking procedure, God gives us His gifts to invest by serving others. When we serve others, we make them our friends. Just how they shall receive us into eternal habitations is told us in Matt. 25:34-40. On Judgement Day Christian deeds of mercy will stand as proofs of faith. "Inasmuch as ye have done it unto the least of these My brethren, ye have done it unto Me," Jesus said.

Jesus used this story only to commend the wisdom and foresight of the steward, not to recommend his dishonesty. The point is clear. Make your life with God's gifts of grace, time, treasures, and talents an investment for eternity.

— Adapted from *Christ Calls Us to Grow*
Augsburg Publishing House

27. JESUS LOVES CHILDREN

Materials

A short pencil, a long pencil, and various pencils — red, yellow, black, white — and a light brown pencil. A sheet of paper.

Display the short and long pencil. Ask, "Which one stands for a child?" (Invariably, children will answer, "The short one." That answer is wrong. Explain that the longer one represents the child, because it has a longer use. If the answer is given correctly as the long one, then have the children explain the reason why.)

Then show the red, yellow, black, and white pencils. They represent the various races of people in the world. God loved the whole world and sent His Son. (John 3:16)

Show the light brown pencil. This one stands for the Son of God. He came into the world as a true human. He became what we are that we might become what He is (Gal. 4:4-7). We use this "middle color" for Jesus because He didn't come to save only one race but all — black, white, yellow, and others. Jesus is the center of all, the only hope of the world.

When Jesus walked this earth on His way to the cross, He showed His love for children, too (Matt. 18:1-6, Mark 10:13-16). He took them up in His arms and blessed them. (Hold the colored pencils around the "Christ pencil.") He even made children object lessons of faith. Children believe with a humble, simple faith. Jesus said: "Whoever does not receive the kingdom of God like a child [that is, like a child receives it in humble faith] shall not enter it."

Just think! When you are saved as a child, you have a longer time to serve Jesus. Pencils are used to write letters and to do school work. In the hands of dishonest people pencils write lies; they are used to cheat. But in the hands of honest people they are used for good purposes. So when we put our lives in Jesus' hands, they will be always used for good to help others. Let us tell others of Jesus' love and write God's love letters for the world to read. (Write on a piece of paper a part of John 3:16, and give it to another person.)

28. LADDER TO HEAVEN

Materials

A white 4×16'' piece of paper. Fold paper into thirds and then into sixths (accordion fashion, according to diagrams 1 and 2). Cut out letter I and shade black as in diagrams 3 and 4. The letter I, when turned horizontally, will be an H for heaven (diagram 5). It will become a ladder (diagram 6) and finally be formed into a cross (diagram 7).

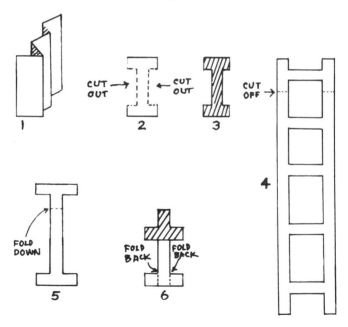

In my hand is a big black letter I. It will tell the story from Gen. 28:10 to 22. This I stands for Jacob. We meet Jacob at the point in his life when he tricked his blind father Isaac and his brother Esau to obtain the birthright and the patriarchal blessing. Esau became angry and planned to kill Jacob. But Rebecca, his mother, warned him. So Jacob fled to Haran to her father's house. This letter I reminds us that Jacob was self-willed and headstrong. This I is black, indicating that this is sin. When we let the I become the most important thing in our lives, we are bound to get into trouble. Sin brings fear and guilt. Jacob felt these as he fled from home. When night came, he was alone under the open sky. He was away from home surroundings and therefore felt that he left the promises of God behind. And since he obtained the birthright by trickery, he could not be sure of God's abiding blessings. Guilty, tired, fearful, he made a pillow of stones and went to sleep. (Turn I on the side, as in sleeping position.)

While he slept, God granted Jacob a vision of heaven. (Turn white side forward and hold to make letter H for heaven.) God spoke to Jacob in a dream. God still loved Jacob and made a way to reveal His love to him.

The revelation in the dream was a ladder reaching to heaven. (Let the H unfold to make a ladder.) Angels were going up and coming down. God Himself was on the top of the ladder; He said, "I am the Lord, the God of Abraham your father and the God of Isaac . . . and by you and your descendants shall all the families of the earth bless themselves."

What did Jacob see with the eyes of faith? (Fold up the ladder to form the letter I again. Bend the top over to form a cross.) Jacob really saw in the vision of faith the Promised One who on the cross made payment for the sins of the whole world. The Bible says: "It does not say, 'And to offsprings,' referring to many; but, referring to one, 'And to your offspring,' which is Christ." (Gal. 3:16)

Jesus referred Nathanael to this event (John 1:51) saying: "Truly, truly, I say to you, you will see heaven opened and the angels of God ascending and descending upon the Son of Man."

So, in the cross of Christ God has reached down to earth. By it God tells the world: "I am reconciled to you, sinful world, because My Son has taken all the guilt of your sins to Himself and died your hell-deserving death."

Like Jacob's our daily walk of life is stained with sin. But we can come to God in Christ's name and merits by way of the cross and find God full of grace and love. "If anyone is in Christ, he is a new creation; the old has passed away, behold, the new has come" (2 Cor. 5:17). This is God's glorious working in the man who uses His ladder to heaven.

— Amplified and adapted from
Object Talks With Paper and Scissors
Standard Publishing

29. LET YOUR LIGHT SHINE

Materials

A flashlight stuffed with rags on which are written greed, pride, disobedience, lust, gossiping, coveting, impurity, etc.

Flashlight batteries, labeled Power of God.

I have a flashlight in my hand. What is a flashlight for? Yes, it is to give light in dark places. When we want to use a flashlight, we must push the button on. I push this one, and it does not go on.

Let us see what is wrong with it. (Open and pull out the rags one by one and display them so that the words can be seen, and comment on the sins mentioned.) This flashlight illustrates what is wrong with all people — we are full of sin by nature. In Is. 64:6 we read: "we are all as an unclean thing, and all our righteousnesses are as filthy rags . . . and our iniquities . . . have taken us away" (KJV). By nature we cannot serve God because we are spiritually dead and cut off from God's light and life.

The Spirit of God goes to work on sinful man. Through the Law He works sorrow over sin, and through the Gospel He works faith in Christ. Here are the batteries which this flashlight needs. I've labeled them "Power of God." It says in Rom. 1:16 "I am not ashamed of the Gospel; it is the power of God for salvation to every one who has faith." The Holy Spirit calls and converts by the Gospel. (Insert batteries and then push the button on.) Now this flashlight is useful.

When Christ comes into our hearts by His Spirit, we are brought to shine for Christ in the dark places of this world. Jesus once said: "You are the light of the world. . . . Let your light so shine before men that they may see your good works and give glory to your Father who is in heaven." (Matthew 5:14-16)

We are to be very careful not to obscure the light by giving in to sin. (Place a rag over the light and name the sin.) When this rag is placed over the light, it becomes dim. When we give in to sinful habits (place another rag and name the sin) our light is dimmed more and more. Before long others cannot see that we belong to Christ. If you miss church, fight on the street, and damage your neighbor's property, can others tell that you belong to Christ? Christ puts His Christians in the dark places of the world to shine for Him and light the way for others. Live for Him a life that is true, and speak of Christ to others.

As this flashlight is useless unless it has its batteries, so a person is useless to God and lost in sin unless he has faith in Jesus Christ. The power of God in Christ makes believers new creatures. They live to shine for Him. A child's hymn says:

"This little Gospel light of mine,
I'm going to let it shine all the time."

I think of Matthew (Matt. 9:4), Zacchaeus (Luke 19:1-10), and the blind man (John 9). These found their lives changed from darkness to light in the Lord.

30. LESSON IN RELATIONSHIPS

Materials

A small Bible; magazine pictures of bread, clothing, house, milk, meat. Mount pictures on cardboard, and by varying lengths of ribbon attach them to the Bible at Matthew 6:33. Put the Bible and pictures into a package wrapped as a gift package.

This is a beautiful package, isn't it? This package is special because it has a message from God. It will teach us a lesson in relationships. Let us open it. How wonderful! A Bible! The Bible is God's Word. It brings us the knowledge of salvation through Jesus. (2 Tim. 3:15)

But look, there is more in the package. As I lift the Bible, there are ribbons attached to it which in turn connect with a number of things. (Lift the Bible higher and higher so the items appear one by one.) There is bread. Bread is a gift of God. There is clothing. We can have so many kinds of clothes—for parties, for school, for work, and for church. God is so good to us. There is a house. Houses are beautiful. They make living so comfortable. There is milk, which makes muscles big and strong, and teeth sound and white. There is meat for strength-giving protein.

What does God mean to teach us by these gifts in this package? The Bible is open to Matt. 6:33, "Seek first His kingdom and His righteousness, and all these things shall be yours as well."

God means that when we have Him as our Father by trusting in Jesus, He will give us what we need in life. We are not to put our trust in things like food and clothing, houses, and other material things.

God's Word must come first. Through His Word we find Christ and His righteousness. That is the way into God's kingdom. Then He promises to give what we really need in this life.

In Rom. 8:32 we are told that God did not spare His own Son but gave Him up for us all. Then the apostle Paul asks: "Will He not also give us all the things with Him?" If God gave us the gift of His Son to save us for heaven, He will also give us the ribbons that go with the package, that is, the promise of His temporal care. God never promised to give us our selfish desires—only what we need!

One time Jesus went to the home of Mary and Martha (Luke 10:38-42). Martha was busy preparing food to serve Jesus. Mary sat at Jesus' feet to hear His Word. Martha faulted Jesus for keeping Mary from helping. Jesus corrected Martha, saying: "Martha, Martha, you are anxious and troubled about many things, one thing is needful. Mary has chosen the good portion, which shall not be taken away from her." Here is a lesson in relationships too. First the Word! Then the cares about eating and living can be attended to. Sometimes people miss church and Sunday school because company is coming. Many people find extra jobs on Sunday just to have more of life's things. They fail to hear God's Word. Families are often too busy with meals and TV programs to say family prayers or have family devotions. When we put God's Word first, we will then live by faith in Christ and trust that God will take care of us. We will thank Him for all His gifts and not let the gifts blind our view of the Giver.

I also think of Solomon, who learned the lesson in relationships. (Read 1 Kings 3:5-15.) Solomon asked for spiritual blessings for the praise of God. God's Word was first in his life. God added many temporal blessings to his life.

31. LOVE THAT WILL NOT LET US GO

Materials

Two candles. One candle stands for Christ's light, the other for the believer. When the believer-candle is blown out (or snuffed out with wet fingers), one immediately holds the flame of the Christ-candle an inch or two above the smoking wick. The flame jumps to the blown-out candle. (The carbon in the smoke burns, causing the flame to ignite the wick.)

Here is a flaming candle. It reminds us that Jesus Christ is the Light of the world (John 8:12). He gives His saving light to men (John 1:9), as is shown by the lighting of this candle. But it happens sometimes that a person is tempted by the devil, the world, or his own flesh, and his faith wavers, flickers, or is blown out. Can you think of anyone in the Bible who lost faith for a time?

Yes, there was King David, who was tempted by his own flesh. He committed adultery with Bathsheba and then murdered her husband. Faith apparently vanished from his sinful heart. (2 Sam. 11)

Then we think of the apostle Peter. He was tempted by the devil and the world to deny Christ. In a moment of weakness he denied Him. Faith vanished from his heart! (Luke 22:54-62)

Yet in these two Bible accounts we recall that God yearned with great love to forgive them. God brought them back. Let us watch the candles closely. I will blow out the believer-candle to represent loss of faith, and then hold the Christ-candle 1 or 2 inches above it. What happened? The flame jumped to the wick of the blown-out candle. God's love in Christ is that way. He is not willing that any should perish.

So with King David. God sent Nathan to remind him of his great sin and to call him to repentance. David repented, and Nathan said: "The Lord also has put away your sin; you shall not die" (2 Sam. 12:13). God kindled the flame of faith again in David's heart. (See Ps. 32 and 51)

To Peter Jesus promised: "I have prayed for you that your faith may not fail; and when you have turned again, strengthen your brethren" (Luke 22:32). Peter was very sorry that he had denied Christ. He wept tears of repentance. He remembered all that Jesus said. He knew there was love enough to forgive him. On Easter Sunday Jesus appeared to Peter, surely to assure him of forgiveness. His flame of faith too, was rekindled. After that Peter was more careful not to let the devil and the world blow out his faith. He did strengthen the brethren. He preached. He witnessed. He wrote epistles. Read what he says about resisting the devil in faith. (1 Peter 5:8-10)

In fact all of Luke 15 tells us of love that will not let us go. The yearning love of God is pictured in the seeking shepherd, the searching woman, and the waiting father. The flame of saving love jumps to save the lost and enlighten with faith.

When sinners experience the great love of God, it moves them to live closer to God in Christ's light, shunning sin and striving to serve God. King David and Peter did it. It will work that way for us, too, when we realize how great is God's love in Christ and that He will not let us go. (Rom. 6:1-4)

A person can be lost by drawing away from Christ in unbelief. When this candle is blown out and moved far away, the flame cannot jump that far. Judas, for one, was lost in unbelief. Yet the love of God yearns to forgive the penitent. "A bruised reed He will not break, and a dimly burning wick He will not quench." (Is. 42:3)

32. LOVE, THE GREATEST VIRTUE

Materials

An 8½″×11″ piece of white paper. Fold and cut out a heart to represent love (figures 1 and 2). Then cut according to figure 3. As illustrated in figure 4, the cross stands for faith and the anchor for hope. Figure 5 shows the final heart when the cross and anchor points are cut off.

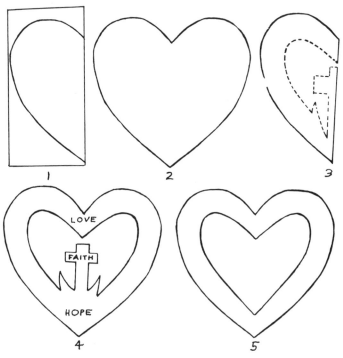

This piece of paper will present to us a great lesson on love. So I cut out a heart. In 1 Corinthians 13 we have the love chapter of the Bible. The word love means an intelligent, Christian love—love that is self-giving. The apostle Paul states that Christian love gives value to all Christian acts and that it has values all its own. At the end of the chapter he says: "So faith, hope, love abide, these three; but the greatest of these is love."

I will cut this heart in such a way as to illustrate all three virtues. The cross in the center stands for faith. Faith is trusting in the Christ of the cross for personal salvation. Notice how the cross with the bottom of the heart, forms an anchor. An anchor is a symbol of Christian hope. Faith that is set upon its heavenly goal is hope.

We wonder why the apostle Paul said that the greatest of these virtues is love. So we think of it this way. Faith is very personal, isn't it? You have it, and it blesses you with spiritual life. Hope is personal too. But love affects others. Love is greatest, first of all, because of its human involvement. When you have faith and hope, you also have a heart of love. You are concerned about the welfare of others. So where there is bitterness, you show forgiveness. Where there is hate, you show kindness. Where people don't know Christ, there you tell others of Him.

But there is another sense in which love is the greatest. When you and I reach heaven, we won't need faith anymore. We will see Christ face to face. (Cut off the cross part, figure 4.) Also, when we get to heaven our hope will be fulfilled. (Cut off the anchor points, figure 4). Now what alone remains? It is the heart. Perfect love makes heaven heaven. Notice that the heart is white. It stands for the perfection and purity of heaven. Already now this purity is given to believers to share with others.

Just as I can now see you through this heart, so God sees us as His own who are saved to show love.

Christian love is born in the hearts of those who know Jesus Christ as Savior from sin and eternal death. It is a Spirit-worked glow of coming glory. Jesus spoke of Christian love in the Upper Room (John 13 and 15). Early Christians practiced it in a special way (Acts 4:32-36). The apostle John became known as the apostle of love because he showed it and encouraged it in his epistles.

33. MONEY MISUSED

Materials

A cross with a magnet attached to the base, a nickel, and a few nails. Test the strength of the magnet through the thickness of the coin with the weight of the nails. When the coin is placed between the magnet and nail, the magnetic current is reduced so that the nail drops.

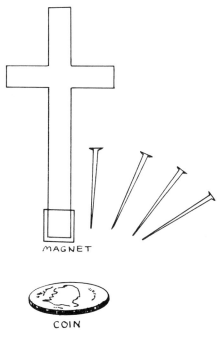

MAGNET

COIN

Here is a cross with a magnet at its base. (Hold up cross.) It reminds me of Jesus' words: "And I, when I am lifted up from the earth, will draw all men to Myself (John 12:32). Jesus came to pay for the sins of the world and to draw all people to Himself. I draw this magnet through these nails. Look how they cling to the cross! The magnet draws them. Look again! Some nails are held up by touching just the nails in contact with the magnet. This shows us that those who belong to Jesus bring others to Him. Living and serving in His kingdom is life's purpose.

Here is a coin. Let us see what happens when this coin comes between the magnet and the nail. The nail just cannot be held up. It drops off. Similarly, when a person trusts earthly riches or himself, he rejects the true riches of Christ.

One time a rich young man came to Jesus (Matt. 19: 16-26). He wanted to know what to do to inherit eternal life. He had been trying to be saved by keeping God's commandments. So Jesus directed him to the commandments, underscoring "Love your neighbor as yourself." The young man boasted of having kept all the commandments from his youth up.

Jesus asked him to sell all his possessions, give the money to the poor, and come and follow Him. Right here Jesus showed the young man that he was not loving God above all else. He had been idolizing his possessions as his god. This made him guilty of breaking all the commandments. Jesus wanted to save him, but trust in money came between him and his Savior just as a coin comes between the magnet and the nail. The young man went away sorrowful. He missed life's greatest purpose — to find Christ and to bring others to Him. Anyone who trusts riches or possessions and makes them his god, cannot belong to God. Trust in Christ is the only way. When we belong to God, we will let Him rule us. We will strive to walk the way of all His commands. We will not trust our money but put it in God's service. (Hold coin in hand and then give it to someone.) We give some of our money for mission work and charity to help others find life's purpose in Christ. We use some of our money for personal needs. But to belong to God means to entrust ourselves and the use of our money to His purposes. His purposes always include drawing others through the cross of Christ.

Illustrate again the power of the magnet holding on to a nail, with other nails holding on to the first nail.

We don't know whether the rich young man came back to Christ. Right now it's most important that you are trusting in Christ, and living under His power. In fact, as we look at a coin, it says in effect: "Don't trust me; I corrode; I can be lost; I am only temporal." It says on the coin itself "In God we trust." (Read 1 Timothy 6:17-19; 5:8-10 for proper use of riches.)

34. NEW HEARTS FOR OLD

Materials

Make two black hearts of cardboard. Hinge, and lock with a small padlock (figure 1). Use three other keys besides the one which fits the lock. Label one Good Works, another Knowledge, another Prayer, and the right key Faith in Christ. Mark reverse side at label of the right key with a black cross. The label on the right key should be an envelope containing the white pieces which are placed on the heart when opened (figure 2). The pieces should be cut as illustrated and have in red letters these words: *faith, peace, prayer, love, joy,* and *good works.* One piece is a picture of Christ for the center. (These can be attached with straight pins.) As an added effect, use brown crayon to write a number of the sins listed in Matt. 15:19 on the outside of the heart.

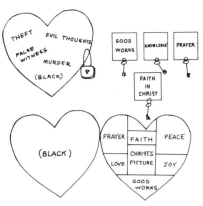

101

Look at this heart — so black and awful looking! It stands for the heart of man by nature. The Bible says of it: "The heart is deceitful above all things and desperately corrupt" (Jer. 17:9). Jesus said: "Out of the heart come evil thoughts, murder, adultery, fornication, theft, false witness, slander" (Matt. 15:19 RSV). The penalty for such a depraved heart is clearly given: "Death spread to all men because all men sinned" (Rom. 5:12). The heart of all men is locked to all good by nature.

(Give four children the keys in advance of the presentation. At this point have those with the three wrong keys come forth and try to unlock the heart. Comment after each try.) Some people try good works. They feel that doing a little good now and then makes them right with God. But working will not save anyone. "Not because of the deeds done by us in righteousness" (Titus 3: 5). Some try knowledge. They think that all man need do to get better is to keep on learning in the field of human wisdom. Knowledge cannot save (1 Cor. 1:20). Then there are others who try a little prayer. But praying will not open the locked heart of man because man's iniquities have separated him from God so that God cannot hear (Is. 59:2). Here is another key marked Faith in Christ. It is marked with a black cross, for Christ took the sins of the whole world upon Himself and died to save it. Christ comes with forgiveness and invites men to believe. This key unlocks the heart of man.

Now the heart is open. What a dismal place Christ comes to! But He comes to make hearts new by renewing them. He takes His place at the center of the heart. (Place His picture in the center.) He brings a whole package of spiritual blessings. He gives believers a continuing faith to trust Him. (Place all the blessings as illustrated.) Peace comes from faith. When the fear of punishment is

102

taken away, there is peace with God (Rom. 5:1). Joy is the settled attitude that is not disturbed by the trials and problems of life. Love is the giving of oneself to the things of God. Prayer is the voice of faith talking with God in the Savior's name. Good works come as a fruit of faith. They cannot save; they follow faith (Eph. 2:8-10). Now look at this side of the heart. It is made new by faith in Christ. The red letters remind us that these blessings come to us through Jesus' blood.

Notice the other side of the heart. It is still black. It is unregenerate! This is the "old Adam" that clings to believers on this side of heaven. Thus a Christian is a saint and sinner at the same time. That is what the apostle Paul meant when in Rom. 7:18-19 he said: "I know that nothing good dwells within me, that is, in my flesh. I can will what is right, but I cannot do it. For I do not do the good I want, but the evil I do not want is what I do." Paul was talking about the inner conflict between the "old" sinner-self and the "new" saint-self in Christ. In heaven there will be perfect renewal. On this side of heaven, we face conflict and continually need the power of God in the means of grace — the Gospel and the Sacraments — so that faith will be kept steadfast and the heart open to the renewing power of Christ. The daily prayer should be:

> Renew me, O eternal Light,
> And let my heart and soul be bright,
> Illumined with the light of grace
> That issues from Thy holy face.

35. THE POWER OF GOD'S WORD

Materials

Two tumblers, two candles, two tablespoonfuls of baking soda, clear water, vinegar, black ink, and matches. Put the candles on small jar covers, waxed in tightly, and set them inside the tumblers. The candles should be short enough to let the flame be below the top of the glasses. Put a small amount of water in each glass and to one glass add the soda. Put the vinegar in a third glass or bottle and discolor it with black ink.

We will give these glasses names. One we will call Tim and the other Tom. When they were infants their parents brought them to Jesus in Baptism: for "the washing of regeneration and renewal in the Holy Spirit" (Titus 3:5). By the power of Baptism spiritual life was put in their hearts. (Light the candles.) These boys heard about Jesus from their parents as they grew into childhood, and soon they went to Sunday school, and in time church-going became more meaningful too.

But as with all Christians, there is the evil of the world, the flesh, and the devil that tries to win them away from Jesus. (Show the glass of black vinegar to represent the evils of life.)

Both Tim and Tom experienced the evils of life. They had playmates who did not love Jesus. Their playmates didn't go to church and Sunday school, nor did they hear about Jesus in their homes. They were full of mischief and appeared to have a lot of fun. In fact these boys made fun of Tim and Tom for going to Sunday school and church. They called them "sissies." Before long Tom aped their ways and was often missing from church and Sunday school. He didn't care to read his Bible at home. When he was in church, he dreamed away the time instead of listening. He became a problem in Sunday school. Soon he disliked the teacher and set his heart against religion. Tim loved God's Word and made every effort to practice it.

Which boy remained strong? We will pour this "evil" into each glass. I pour it into Tom. (Tom is the one with the soda.) What do we see? It is foaming. Evil really became a part of him. Now the light went out. Poor Tom! He reminds me of Peter and Judas. Will Tom get another chance to be born again?

Now I pour the same "evil" into Tim. He still "burns" for Jesus!

What made the difference? It was the hearing of God's Word that kept Tim strong amid evil. God promises to keep us as we hear His Word. If we forsake His Word, then evil overcomes us easily.

There is a real Tim in the Bible who loves God's Word and remains strong. We read about him in 2 Timothy 3:14-17. The apostle Paul admonished Timothy to continue in God's Word, which he learned as a child. God's Word was able to instruct him for salvation by faith in Christ and to train him in holy living. Timothy was an evangelist, who let his light shine for Jesus.

Jesus wants us to keep "burning," for only by a living faith are we saved. As faith continues, it shows itself in our living. Jesus once said: "Let your light so shine before men that they may see your good works and give glory to your Father who is in heaven." (Matthew 5:16) Do you love God's Word?

— Amplified and adapted from *See It! Object Lessons*
Zondervan Publishing House

36. RIGHT WITH GOD

Justification by Faith

Materials

A set of ornamental scales. One white box labeled *God's Holiness*. One smaller box, gray with black heart pasted to it, with extra black hearts inside. Another white box, the same size as the first, labeled *Christ*. Put a red cross on it. (The white boxes should be weighted in advance to balance the scales, allowing for the weight of the small gray box so the scales finally balance perfectly.) Index cards with numbers for Commandments I, V, and VIII.

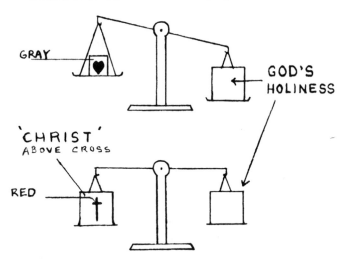

Here is a set of beautiful golden scales. These scales will stand for God's justice. Every person in the world must be weighed in God's scales of justice. I place this white box (God's holiness) on one side. God is perfectly holy. Justice is God's holiness in action.

Now I place another smaller box on the other side. This box stands for man. What do you observe? The scale is out of balance! God's holiness outweighs man 100 percent, or as far as the scale will go. The problem is not that God is too holy but that man is so sinful. This little black heart reminds us of God's diagnosis of every man in Romans 3:10-18 RSV. Some things are mentioned, as: "None is righteous, no, not one . . . no one seeks for God," and man's throat, tongue, and lips are full of bitterness and cursing, and "their feet are swift to shed blood." These are sins especially against the First, Eighth, and Fifth Commandments.

What will make the scales balance? Some people feel that all you need is to do the best you can, and you will be on right terms with God. (Hold up card for Commandment I.) They seek after God now and then, perhaps at Christmas and Easter. (Place the card on the "man side" of the scale.) It does not make the scale balance in man's favor. Why? Is it not because people do not seek God perfectly enough? Even when at worship, do we give God the perfect attention of our heart, soul, and mind? Don't other thoughts crowd in, like the Sunday dinner, the afternoon plans, and the feeling of being bored with God's Word?

Who will lay claim to perfect speech about his neighbor? (Place card for Commandment VIII on the scale.) Haven't we spoken unkind words? Haven't we gossiped? This commandment fails also to balance the scales in our favor.

108

We know that murder is wrong. (Place the card for Commandment V on the scale.) So a lot of people think that as long as they have not murdered anyone they have kept the Fifth Commandment. The Bible says that hating someone is the same as murder in the eyes of God (1 John 3:15). It's so easy to harbor hate toward the "over-strict parents," the "tough teacher," the "bossy spouse." The way we keep this commandment also fails to balance the scales in our favor.

The placing of all the rest of the commandments on the scale, poorly kept by man's puny efforts, would not balance the scales in man's favor either. The scales of God's justice say emphatically: "You are weighed in the balances and found wanting!" This verdict is said to every man: "All have sinned and fall short of the glory of God" (Rom. 3:23 RSV). (Show the other black hearts from the gray box, which stand for the fact expressed in 3:23.) Let us see ourselves on those scales right now. "No human being will be justified in His sight by works of the Law, since through the Law comes knowledge of sin." (Rom. 3: 20)

God knew that man could do nothing by himself to get right with God. So God did it all. God sent His Son to keep the Law perfectly for every person. On the cross He gave His life as a payment for the sins of the world. The red cross on this "Christ box" reminds us that it took the shedding of His precious blood to earn a righteous-ness which could be credited to sinners. Rom. 3:21-22 says, "But now the righteousness of God has been mani-fested apart from Law . . . the righteousness of God through faith in Jesus Christ for all who believe." When a sinner admits that he is lost and looks in faith to Christ for salvation, God credits Christ's holiness and righteous-ness to his account. It is asking Christ to come on the scale with him. (Place the Christ box on the scale.) Now it balances perfectly.

The act of God in declaring sinners righteous for Christ's sake is called justification by faith. It makes a believing person right with God and fit for heaven. In fact Christ's righteousness perfectly covers the sinner, just as I put the Christ box over the sinner box. In Christ alone there is refuge through the covering of sin.

The apostle Paul further expresses this thought, saying: "They are justified by His grace as a gift, through the redemption which is in Christ Jesus, whom God put forward as an expiation [covering] by His blood" (Rom. 3: 24-25 RSV). Then he makes the grand conclusion in 3:28, "For we hold that a man is justified by faith apart from works of Law."

I place the commandments, which could not balance the scales in our favor, on the other side. God accepts them because we are His children, not because we are so perfect. As believers we always strive to do better works to praise God more. Good works follow faith. Salvation comes by faith in the works of Christ alone.

37. SABBATH DAY, OR HOLY DAY?

Materials

A shadow box with detachable back. On the shadow part write the words *Saturday, Rules, Rest* (Sabbath), *Ceremonial Law*. On the back center part write *Moral Law*, and attach pictures of worship occasions such as family worship, public worship, private worship. Make a red cross on the reverse side.

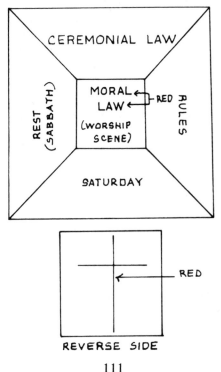

A shadow box is a special way of displaying something. It gives depth to the item. We will let this shadow box teach us something very special about worship.

God gave the Ten Commandments at Mount Sinai through Moses. We can read about that in Ex. 19 and 20. When God gave the worship commandment, He encased it in a shadow-box frame. The shadow part was a part of the ceremonial law. It meant that a specific day was necessary, the seventh. Strict rules were given, too. The people had to keep that day as a rest day and not do any work (Ex. 20:10). It was a time of spiritual reflection on God's mercies and help (Deut. 5:15). This was the moral part of the worship commandment.

The Sabbath Day as a rest day was a type of the spiritual rest that Jesus Christ would bring by His redemptive work on the cross. (Show red cross on reverse side.) When Jesus did this, the ceremonial law was fulfilled and thus the rules relating to a particular day as the Sabbath and to absolute physical rest no longer applied.

We read about this in Col. 2:16-17. The apostle Paul explained it this way: "Let no one pass judgment on you in questions of food and drink or with regard to a festival or a new moon or a Sabbath. These are only a shadow of what is to come; but the substance belongs to Christ." (Detach the shadow part with the ceremonial law and show only the back part with the moral law).

New Testament believers are not bound to the ceremonial rules. Only the moral part applies as a continual act of worship. New Testament believers, who worship God in spirit and in truth, worship at three altars. They worship at the heart altar continually by a living faith in Jesus Christ. They worship at the home altar daily as they read the Bible and pray together or privately. They worship at the church altar regularly.

The choice of the day is left to Christian freedom, but a day must be agreed on for public worship, as the Bible commands (Heb. 10:25). Significantly, the early Christians chose Sunday, the first day of the week, as the day for public worship since Jesus rose from the dead on Sunday, and the Holy Spirit was poured out at the first Pentecost on Sunday. (See also 1 Cor. 16:1-2 and Rev. 1: 10.)

New Testament keeping of this commandment is an act of worship, as the response of the believer's total life to the love of God. Out of love for God believers gladly hear His Word and live according to it. Believers who worship all week at the heart altar and home altar worship best at the church altar. The worship day is a holy day of public praise and hearing of God's Word.

God made the world in six days and rested on the seventh. He could have done it in a second's time. Yet God does His creating over a 6-day period. This became an object lesson to man when God instituted the Sabbath. It meant: "If I, the Almighty God, rested after six days, how much more do you, puny man, need rest to keep your spiritual balance!" The Old Testament arrangement still is our spiritual refreshment. But the specific parts of the ceremonial law are no longer binding. We are free to have public worship on any day of the week. We show that God is worth everything when we with loving hearts keep the flame of worship burning at the three altars.

38. SAVED TO SERVE

Materials

A mirror, a clear window glass, a small, standing, gold-colored cross, and a silver coin.

I have a clear window glass in my hand. A few of you may look through it. What do you see? Yes, you see others through it.

I now have a mirror in my hand. Who wants to look into it? What do you see? Yes, you see only yourself.

What makes the big difference in the two pieces of glass? The difference between the window glass and the mirror is that the mirror has a bit of silver behind the glass, and it reflects your face. An old rabbi once taught a lesson to a miser by having him look into a mirror. He said: "When a little silver is added, you cease to see others and see only yourself."

It was that way with a person in the Bible (Gen. 13). His name was Lot. Lot was selfish. Abraham and Lot had to part company because their herds were too large to graze together. Abraham gave Lot the first choice. He chose the best land. He liked the things of the world more than the things of God. When a man serves himself, he is worshiping the worst idol of all.

On the other hand Abraham loved God and set his heart on the treasures of heaven. He believed God's promises, and it was counted to him for righteousness (Gen. 15:6, Gal. 3:14). Abraham set his heart on the promised Christ. (Show cross.) When a man has Christ, he is eternally rich. Abraham was blessed by God also with temporal riches. But as Abraham kept his eyes of faith on his real riches, he did not let temporal riches spoil him. He rather used them to help others. He looked at life as through a window. (Place cross in front of window glass.) He saw the needs of others through the Savior who was to come. While it is no crime to be rich, it is bad to be rich and not have the right heart toward riches. Abraham had the right heart, for his heart was set on Christ. He also gave a tithe to the Lord. (Gen. 14:18-20)

Instead of letting our lives revolve around ourselves and using God's gifts to serve ourselves (like silver on the mirror), let us use our silver and gold (show coin) to bless the lives of others. Money helps us share the Gospel of the true riches with others. Let God use our self, service, and substance. Like Abraham, realize that we are saved to serve.

> Take my silver and my gold,
> Not a mite would I withhold;
> Take myself and I will be
> Ever, only, all for Thee.

39. SEEDS OF BLESSING

Materials

Two saucers
Apple cut in quarters
Seeds removed from an apple

(Hold saucers before the group, one in each hand.) If you had the choice of the fruit on this saucer (extend saucer) or the seeds on this other saucer (extend it), which would you choose? Will John and Mary please come here. Which do you choose, John? Which do you choose, Mary? (Let the children take their choices. Invariably they will take the fruit. If they choose the seeds, have them explain the reason, and lead to the application.) Well, you chose the fruit over the seeds. Why? You say that the fruit tastes better, or that it satisfies your hunger better than seeds. Do the rest of you agree with them?

Suppose you had chosen the seeds. What use could you make of them? Yes, plant them. Then in 6 or 8 years you would have not just one apple but bushels of them. You can count the seeds in an apple, but you can't count the apples in one seed. What does this mean? An apple tree may grow from a single seed. We cannot know how many apples one tree will bear year after year.

Did you ever hear of Johnny Appleseed? He was an American pioneer who about the year 1800 traveled hundreds of miles through Pennsylvania, Ohio, and Indiana. He wore a coffee sack for a shirt and a saucepan for a hat. He carried a Bible and a package of apple seeds. He spread the Word and planted apple seeds. He thought of the future and of service to others. He denied himself enjoyments of the present for the sake of the future. For many years afterwards every apple tree in that area was a reminder of the thoughtfulness of this man.

Many people are interested only in things that they can enjoy at the moment. Their chief concern is to make themselves happy in the present. They do not care about God's long-range plan—what He wants them to do during their lifetime or how He wants them to prepare for the next life. They live only for today.

Think of Esau (Gen. 25:29-34; Heb. 12:16-17). He chose a bowl of soup, and forfeited his birthright. In Abraham's descendants, through Joseph and Judah, the birthright carried with it the spiritual promise of the coming Savior and future blessings for many people. It read like this: "By you and your descendants shall all the families of the earth be blessed." Esau is called a profane person for making such a bad choice.

Or think of Pontius Pilate. When Jesus stood on trial before him, Pilate had the choice of things for the present or of things for his eternal future. He thought only of his popularity and his earthly position. He failed to see the future blessings in Christ. Jesus plainly stated that His kingdom was not of this world, but one which was eternal. (John 18:28-40)

Or we might think of the parable of the Ten Virgins (Matt. 25). Five were foolish because they made no preparation for the future. The five wise virgins prepared. They looked ahead.

Let us look ahead. Let us use the seed of the Word of God. Then we remember this Bible verse: "Look not to the things that are seen but to the things that are unseen; for the things that are seen are transient, but the things that are unseen are eternal." (2 Cor. 4:18 RSV)

We could not see the apples in the seeds, could we? But don't we all agree that there are more apples in the seeds than what you saw on the saucer and enjoyed for the moment? The apple on the saucer is gone. The seeds, if planted, would produce many more apple trees and apples in the future. How much more is the seed of God's Word a blessing! It brings us all the blessings of Jesus Christ, having the promise of the life that is now and that which is to come. Let us think also of others. When we choose the seeds of blessing, we have blessings to share with others. We can share with others the good news that Jesus delivers from eternal death and gives eternal life to all who believe.

— Adapted from J. E. De Golia
Object Lessons . . . Using Common Things
Scripture Press, 1954

40. SHOWING FORTH CHRIST'S DEATH IN COMMUNION

Materials

An 8½″×11″ piece of white paper. Cut out wafer and chalice as illustrated. Fold as illustrated and make a cross.

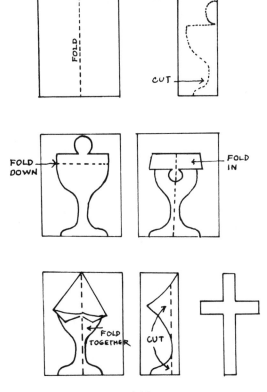

This white piece of paper will teach us some grand truths about Holy Communion. I fold this paper and cut it (illustration 1). This shows us the wafer and the chalice. The wafer is properly called a "host" from a Latin word meaning "victim." The wafer is made of unleavened bread. When Jesus was with His disciples on Maundy Thursday before going to the cross, He used unleavened bread in Holy Communion. We read in Matt. 26:26: "Now as they were eating, Jesus took bread and blessed and broke it, and gave it to the disciples and said, 'Take, eat; this is My body.'" Jesus offered His holy body on the cross as the victim for the sins of the world.

The chalice stands for the other part of Holy Communion. Wine was used in the Passover celebration. Jesus used some of the wine, as we read: "And He took a cup, and when He had given thanks He gave it to them, saying, 'Drink of it, all of you; for this is My blood of the covenant, which is poured out for many for the forgiveness of sins'" (Matt. 26:27-28 RSV). Jesus shed His holy, precious blood in His death on the cross. The body and blood of Christ are the invisible part of Holy Communion.

I fold the wafer and chalice and cut it (illustration 2). What do you see? It is a cross that stands for Christ's cross upon which His body hung in death. This reminds us of the grand truth that Jesus is present with His true body and blood in Holy Communion. This truth is called the real Presence of Christ in Communion. It is so because Jesus, the God-man, declared it so. The real Presence of Christ was settled in that Upper Room when Jesus said, "This *is*." Wherever Holy Communion is observed according to Christ's institution, He is there under the visible elements of bread and wine with His body and blood. Through the invisible body and blood God brings comfort and strength to believers. In this special way

Jesus comes to abide in His believers. He is closer to them than if they were leaning upon His shoulder, like the apostle John in the Upper Room.

Also, those who partake of Holy Communion make an act of confession of faith. The pledge of forgiveness by His body and blood is His special gift to comfort believers and strengthen their faith. Living to confess Christ is the believers' gift to Him. (Show cross again.) The very fact that believers partake of Holy Communion is a public declaration of their faith. Every communicant is by that act saying: "I believe that Jesus died for me long ago on Calvary, and I believe that He is the only Savior of the world. I will, by my life and lips, show forth His death until He comes." And we have God's assurance: "As often as you eat this bread and drink the cup, you proclaim the Lord's death until He comes." (1 Cor. 11:26 RSV)

The very truth that Jesus is present with His body and blood in Holy Communion gives believers strength and power to show forth His death.

41. SIN'S POWER BROKEN

Materials

Black carpet cord and scissors to which a picture of
Jesus with a cross on the back is attached
One thin black thread

(Ask a child to come forward.) You know about
Adam and Eve in the Garden of Eden. The devil came to
the garden to tempt Adam and Eve. They listened to the
devil, and they sinned. (Begin wrapping the heavy thread
around the child at elbow level.) Adam and Eve were
bound by sin in a terrible bondage. They were bound by
fear, sorrow, and death. Their lives became miserable
with sin, and they could not serve God.

(Address the child as you keep winding the cords
around.) Did you ever feel hateful and then hit someone?
Did you ever wish for something so much that you
cheated to get it? One sin leads to another. Stealing leads
to lying to cover up. Disobeying parents and teachers
leads to delinquency. Sin is that way—it brings bondage,
fear, sorrow, guilt, and death. Everyone who comes into
the world is bound by the cords of sin. "You were dead
through the trespasses and sins" (Eph. 2:1 RSV). Jesus
once said, "Everyone who commits sin is a slave to sin."
(John 8:34)

You cannot serve God all bound up like this, can
you? How can you get free? (Ask the child to try to
break himself loose. Make sure you have enough strands
to make it impossible to break loose.)

I will tell you how you can be set free. I have scissors in my hand. Do you believe that the scissors can cut the threads? Do you want to be set free? Now look at the picture attached to the scissors. It is a picture of Jesus. He came to set us free from the bondage of sin. Already in the Garden of Eden God promised victory in the woman's Seed (Gen. 3:15). Adam and Eve were set free from sin's penalty and power when they believed. When Jesus told the people about sin's bondage, He added: "So if the Son makes you free, you will be free indeed." (John 8:36)

Now I cut the thread and set you free. You are free to use your arms and hands and your entire self in the service of Christ, who freed you. But remember! The devil doesn't want you to be free and serve Christ. He will try hard to catch you in his cords. (Put thinner thread around, a strand or two.) The devil tempts you to lie and cheat. So what do you do? You watch for the devil's black cords, and with the loving desire to serve Christ, you break them before they wrap you in bondage. (Child should break loose from the threads.) This is called living in repentance. We watch for sin, and we repent of it, asking Christ to forgive our sins. We then fight sin, resisting already its beginnings. In this way we can be kept free to serve Christ with willing newness of life.

Christ set all of us free at a great cost. (Show cross on back of picture.) He died on the cross and defeated sin, death, and the devil. He rose again to prove it. As we trust Him to set us free and keep us free, we give our best efforts to serve Him. This is our reasonable service. Christ frees us from the penalty of sin. He gives us daily power over sin, and one day He will free us from the presence of sin when He takes us to heaven.

42. SPIRITUAL STOP SIGN

Materials

A cardboard stop sign, with the word STOP.

Look at the word STOP letter by letter. It presents a summary of the central teachings in the Bible.

The letter S looks like a serpent, doesn't it? What does that remind us of? Yes, of the devil, who in the form of a serpent led the first man and woman to disobey God. Disobeying God is called "sin," and that word begins with an S. The next letter is T which looks like a cross on which our Savior died to pay for all sins. The letter O reminds us of the open door of the tomb from which Jesus rose. It also reminds us that the door to heaven is open to all who believe in Jesus. All who believe in Jesus as Savior from sin tell it to others. What words meaning "tell" begin with the letter P? They are the words, preach, proclaim, and publish.

Whenever you see the word STOP on a stop sign, think of what the Bible says about being saved from sin by Jesus' death and rising again. Remember that you are to tell others this truth.

Stop signs are placed at crossroads where we consider the direction of travel and also watch for others. God's spiritual stop sign is at the cross-roads of life — at the broad and the narrow ways. The broad way leads to destruction — the narrow way to life. (Matt. 7:13-14)

Every worship service is a stopping from life's busy ways to consider the truths of God and to be empowered to tell others with new zeal. Every Lord's Day is a little Easter, a reminder of the open tomb and open heaven — open through the forgiveness of sins in Jesus. Early Christians worshiped faithfully (Acts 2:42-47). The disciples also stopped to consider the meaning of the Bible message. They knew that Jesus rose. They were engaged in worship. When they received the promised Holy Spirit (Acts 1:8, Acts 2), they went out to tell. (See also Luke 24:34-53.) Peter was here, Philip there, and Paul yonder.

Let us stop and consider the truths of the Bible by faithful Bible study and worship. Let us take time and stop to tell others what the Bible says — how sinners can find forgiveness of sins in Jesus.

— Adapted from *Adventures with God*
Concordia Publishing House, 1966

43. THE FORGIVEN FORGIVE

Materials

A 12-inch white cardboard heart on which the words Selfishness, Jealousy, Wrongs, Revenge, Evil, Envy, Hatred, are written as illustrated (Figure 1). Hinge two half hearts on spots marked. The half heart pieces should be cut so that the word Forgive shows when hinged forward. One side of each half heart should be red so when swung forward the red will be seen (Figure 2). Display the heart with the heart halves swung backwards.

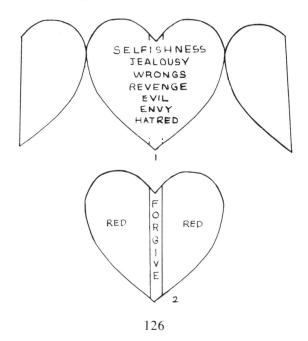

SELFISHNESS
JEALOUSY
WRONGS
REVENGE
EVIL
ENVY
HATRED

1

RED   F O R G I V E   RED

2

This white heart is full of terrible sins. They are sins committed in a family chosen by God to be a bearer of His promises. Sometimes we Christians, who are chosen by God to bear His name into the world, carelessly let sin mar our lives. Many times an unforgiving spirit embitters our lives and the lives of others.

We read about Jacob's sons in Gen. 37:15-36. Joseph became the target for his brothers' offenses. They were very selfish. When Jacob gave Joseph a coat of many colors, they acted selfishly and let jealousy rule them. They wronged Joseph in casting him into the pit and later selling him as a slave. This was their revenge against him for taking their father's favor from them. The brothers thought and practiced evil because of their envy and hatred of him.

How do you think Joseph reacted to all this? Joseph too had the same things in his heart, didn't he? The Bible says that the old nature of sin clings to God's children and burdens their hearts and lives. Well, Joseph did not let these sins rule him. He found forgiveness in the promised Savior. (Hinge the heart halves forward.) Joseph remembered that God promised a Savior. He trusted that promise, and his sins were covered. When God covers a person's sins with the blood of His Son, his heart becomes forgiving. In Gen. 50:15-21 we read that when Joseph's brothers asked him to forgive them, he forgave and showed his forgiveness by helping them.

Many times people say, "I will forgive you but I will not forget." That is not forgiveness. Forgiveness acts in kindness.

An unforgiving heart is really an unbelieving heart. The heart that really believes in God's forgiveness for Christ's sake also forgives others.

To prove that a forgiven sinner forgives, Jesus once told a parable about forgiveness (Matt. 18:21-35). He made a special application of forgiveness, following the giving of the Lord's Prayer (Matt. 6:9-15), to show how important it is to forgive others. Paul wrote: "Be kind to one another, tenderhearted, forgiving one another, as God in Christ forgave you." (Eph. 4:32)

Let us be like Joseph and live forgivingly. As we keep our sins covered with the blood of Christ, they are kept from ruling us. The new life of faith controls us in a life of forgiveness when we realize what it means to have a heart covered with Christ's blood. "He [Jesus Christ] is the expiation [covering] for our sins, and not for ours only but also for the sins of the whole world" (1 John 2:2). This is our power to be forgiving Josephs.

44. TRANSFORMED CHRISTIANS

Materials

A lump of coal, mothballs, perfume, and a phonograph record with a Christian hymn.

This lump of coal will represent the natural condition of man. Coal is dead vegetable matter. The substance was once green and living. But forces of nature buried it deep in the earth, pressing it down, and so it became coal. Adam and Eve, our first parents, had spiritual life in God. But when they sinned against God, they became spiritually dead under the burden of sin. Death passed to all men in that all have sinned.

Coal would stay buried if miners didn't bring it out. So all people would be lost and condemned forever if God had not sent His Son to lift man out of sin's condemnation. Coal in its natural state is only good for burning. Now scientists have found new uses for coal by refining and transforming it. The by-products of coal furnish the basis for many things in life.

For example, here are mothballs. They are pure and white. They are so useful, too. They keep precious garments from being ruined by moths. Believers, who are transformed by the Spirit, become useful to God. They keep society from moral ruin by their good influence. (Matt. 5:13-16)

Here is a bottle of perfume. Believers add a sweet fragrance to life by the kind deeds they do and the helpful words they speak. Prov. 27:9 says: "Ointment and perfume rejoice the heart; so doth the sweetness of a man's friend by hearty counsel." (KJV)

Here is a phonograph record. (If you have a record player, play a part of the record.) Believers are to spread the message of God's love by their songs and testimonies. Also their daily lives are a living record of God's power.

We read of many people in the Bible who experienced this transformation and became useful like mothballs, perfume, and records. I think of John the Baptist (Luke 3), Dorcas (Acts 9:36), Stephen (Acts 6 – 7), Lydia (Acts 16:11-15), Cornelius (Acts 10), and many others who are good examples of living transformed lives.

Now it is our turn. The Holy Spirit has called us to faith for a purpose. Daily ask the Holy Spirit to use you for His purposes. Don't be satisfied just to be lump-of-coal Christians. But as the Bible says: "Be ye transformed by the renewal of your mind, that you may prove what is the will of God, what is good and acceptable and perfect." (Rom. 12:2)

– Adapted from *Object Lessons . . . Using Common Things*
J. E. De Golia, Scripture Press, 1954

45. THREE-IN-ONE GOD

(The Trinity)

Materials

(1) A circle of heavy cardboard or wood painted black, with a hole in center. (2) A fan-shape of cardboard or masonite of same size painted white (with hole in center), upon which are written some attributes of God: *Eternal, All-Powerful, All-Present, All-Knowing, Changeless, Faithful, Just, Gracious, Love.* (Make sure that *Gracious* is between *Just* and *Love.*) In the center, write: *God is a spirit.* Write with green, symbolizing God's eternity. (3) A triangle-circle symbol of the Trinity with the names *Father, Son,* and *Holy Spirit* printed in green letters. Symbol may be in gold or silver color, made of cardboard. (4) A red cross. (5) You will also need a pin and a washer about ½ inch in diameter to insert between "fan shape" and circle back. Make the object as large as you desire. It can be made to be a permanent object lesson for classroom use.

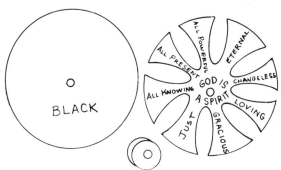

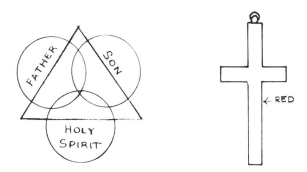

Look at this black circle. This will represent what we know of God by nature. Creation tells us that God exists. So does our conscience. "Ever since the creation of the world His invisible nature, namely, His eternal power and deity, has been clearly perceived in the things that have been made. So they are without excuse" (Rom. 1:20). And: "Their conscience also bears witness." (Rom. 2:15)

The natural knowledge of God, however, only tells us of God's existence and power. This is a frightening, black concept to helpless, sinful man.

God in His Word reveals Himself to mankind as He is in His saving action. (Place fan shape over the black circle.) The Bible tells us that He has the following attributes or qualities (define and explain each of them):

Eternal — Ps. 90:1-2
All-powerful — Gen. 17:1
All-present — Jer. 23:24
All-knowing — Ps. 139:1-4
Changeless — Mal. 3:6
Faithful — 2 Tim. 2:13
Just — Deut. 32:4
Gracious — Exodus 34:6-7
Love — 1 John 4:8
God is a Spirit — John 4:24

132

The Bible also says that God is one in His being or makeup. "Hear, O Israel: The Lord, our God, is one Lord" (Deut. 6:4). And: "There is no God but one" (1 Cor. 8:4). As I give this fan shape a spin, these attributes blend to form one — to remind us that there is only one God, who made heaven and earth and is active in the plan of salvation.

The Bible further reveals God as having three persons. "Go therefore and make disciples of all nations, baptizing them in the name of the Father and of the Son and of the Holy Spirit" (Matt. 28:19). Another verse says: "The grace of the Lord Jesus Christ and the love of God and the fellowship of the Holy Spirit be with you all" (2 Cor. 13:14). See also Matt. 3:16-17. (Show the Trinity symbol and explain — three circles for the three persons joined in one triangle to express the three-in-one God.) (Place behind fan shape on black circle.) Again the fan shape will be given a spin. Watch it closely. What do you see? Yes, you see the names of God's three persons behind the "oneness" of God. It is a sort of optical illusion. This gives us an idea that God is three distinct persons in one divine Being, or Essence. Each person is fully God. A short name for this is Trinity — three-in-one God. Notice that God's revelation is depicted in white to show His holiness.

Now look at some of the attributes of God. God is holy. He is sinless and hates sin. God is just. He gives people what they deserve. By sinning, people deserve eternal death unless something happens to change it. Something did happen. God is love. Love moved God to have pity on sinful people. Love moved the Father to send His Son to become man and take people's sins upon Himself to satisfy His justice. (Place the cross under the attribute "gracious" and explain that God is gracious to

133

sinners for Christ's sake and favors them with forgiveness and pardon.)

When you and I meet God at the foot of the cross, we receive life from God, for the Holy Spirit imparts it by faith. (Move the name of the Holy Spirit downward to show that the Holy Spirit creates faith and gives life through the message of the cross.) Some people think they can come to God on their own terms, but His justice condemns sinners. God's condemnation fell once on His Son when He died on the cross. Coming to God in Him is the only way to life.

When a person believes in Christ, then the attributes of God go into action in the believer's behalf. God is all-present: He is ever near us. God is all-powerful: He can and does protect. God is changeless: He is our unfailing comfort in a changing and decaying world. God is eternal: He is without beginning or end. God is gracious: He daily and richly forgives all sins for Christ's sake.

The Trinity doctrine is far above human understanding. It is for faith to accept. The doctrine of the Trinity is most practical, for it reveals God in His saving action toward sinful man. The Father is like the doctor who writes out the prescription for sinful man's cure. The Son is the loving pharmacist who fills it — with His own precious blood. The Holy Spirit is like the nurse who gives the medicine.

> O blessed Holy Trinity,
> Divine, eternal Unity,
> God Father, Son, and Holy Ghost,
> Be Thou this day my Guide and Host.

You can read about the saving action of the triune God in many sections of the Bible; in fact, it is the central theme of the Bible. Read Rom. 5:1-8; Eph. 1:3-14; John 3:1-18; Is. 48:16-17 as some examples.

46. THE TELEPHONE OF PRAYER

Materials

A toy telephone

This telephone will teach us what true prayer is. (Point to the various parts.)

Think of the mouthpiece. In a telephone conversation we speak with someone we do not see. In prayer we speak with God whom we do not see. Yet we can talk to Him. And He has promised to listen to our prayers because we are His children in Christ Jesus. That makes God our Father. Prayer is heart-to-heart talking to God with the voice of faith.

Think of the earpiece. We can hear God speak to us in His Word. There God tells us to pray to Him (Ps. 50: 15). He tells us that we may confess our sins and ask His forgiveness. He promises to help and protect us. We can talk to God about all our needs. If God did not speak to us in His Word, we could not pray, nor would we know how to pray. The more we study and ponder God's Word the better we can pray.

Now look at the cord that connects the earpiece and the mouthpiece to the line and the power at the central office. It stands for faith, which is our connecting link with God. Prayer is faith talking. Jesus said: "And whatever you ask in prayer you will receive, if you have faith." (Matt. 21:22)

Christ's promise gives the power to prayer, for He said: "Truly, truly, I say to you, if you ask anything of the Father, He will give it to you in My name" (John 16: 23). Through Christ the Holy Spirit also works to empower our prayers, as we read in Rom. 8:26-27: "Likewise the Spirit helps us in our weakness; for we do not know how to pray as we ought, but the Spirit Himself intercedes for us with sighs too deep for words . . . according to the will of God."

When we call someone, we dial the number. When we talk with God, we "dial" J E S U S C H R I S T. To pray in His name means that our prayers gain acceptance because He died on the cross to earn forgiveness for us and to make us God's children. As God's children we let the "Christ desires" fill our prayers. That is praying in Jesus Christ's name.

Almost every home has a telephone. There are also telephones in public places. We are never really far from a telephone. There are, however, places where no telephones are available. But the telephone of prayer is always available. We carry it in our believing hearts. We can talk with God at any time and in any place. Daniel prayed in the lions' den (Dan. 6). Paul and Silas prayed in prison (Acts 16). Jesus prayed in the garden in time of sorrow (Matt. 26:36-46). The Bible says: "I desire then that in every place the men should pray, lifting holy hands without anger or quarreling." (1 Tim. 2:8 RSV)

One time Jesus' disciples asked Him to teach them to pray (Luke 11:1). Jesus gave them the Lord's Prayer (Matt. 6:9-13). Jesus taught that real prayer is talking with God as Father about the things that pertain to His name, His kingdom, and His will. It includes the request for daily bread. It includes our greatest needs for daily life — His forgiveness, His power in temptation, and His deliverance from evil. The Lord's Prayer becomes our guide for talking to God over the telephone of prayer.

Many have learned to use the telephone of prayer. Solomon used it on the occasion of the temple dedication (1 Kings 8; 2 Chron. 6). King David used it for confessing his sins (Ps. 51) and for praise (Ps. 100 and other psalms). Peter used it for thanking God (Acts 4:23-31), as did the lepers (Luke 17:11-19). Let us use that wonderful privilege of prayer faithfully.

47. WHAT CONVERSION IS

Materials

A cup. If possible, use a gray or brown cup to represent "that which is born of the flesh is flesh" (John 3: 6). Place the cup upside down on a table or on your hand.

This cup is upside down. What does this cup lack when it is this way?

Yes, it lacks usefulness. A cup is useful when it is right side up. What else is lacking? Light is lacking. There's only darkness within.

The cup also lacks substance. A cup is made to hold liquids. It cannot hold liquid when it is upside down. This cup illustrates how we all are by nature. We are empty of spiritual life, full of darkness of death, and useless to God.

This cup is the color of earth. It reminds us of what Jesus said about man as he is by nature. He said: "That which is born of the flesh is flesh." (John 3:6)

Jesus Christ came to the world to earn life for all people. He lived a flawlessly useful life, as He kept God's law and fulfilled it for man. He also gave His life as a payment for the penalty of man's sin, which is the darkness of eternal death. Through His death there is light and life for mankind. Through that message of salvation the Holy Spirit is at work turning people around.

This cup cannot turn over by itself. A power from the outside must turn it over. So my hand will represent the power of the Holy Spirit. I turn it over. Now what is in the cup? It receives light. It becomes useful. It holds liquid. (Pour some water into it and take a drink.)

Jesus not only said: "That which is born of flesh is flesh," He also said: "That which is born of the Spirit is spirit." (John 3:6)

Jeremiah once prayed: "Turn Thou me and I shall be turned; for Thou art the Lord, my God" (Jer. 31:18 KJV). It is God who does the converting. Man is powerless to turn around or even help along.

Saul, for example, was like an upside-down cup. One day he was converted by God's power. He became a useful vessel of God. He carried the Water of life to others. We know him as the apostle Paul. (Acts 9)

Let us make this humble confession with Luther:

I believe that I cannot by my own reason or strength believe in Jesus Christ, my Lord, or come to Him; but the Holy Ghost has called me by the Gospel, enlightened me with His gifts, sanctified and kept me in the true faith. . . .

48. WHAT FAITH IS

Materials

Unshelled peanut

Hold the peanut hidden in your hand and approach the class, saying: "I have something very special in my hand. You and I have never seen it before, and we will never see it again. How many believe that I have something like that in my hand? Raise your hand." (Many will not raise their hands because it is so unbelievable.)

Then assure those who did not raise their hands, that you are a Christian teacher, that you stand for God's truth, and that you are telling the truth right now. They may therefore take you at your word. (Most of them will raise their hands. There may still be a few doubters.)

Then shell the peanut and show it to them. "See, it's something we have never seen before. It was hidden in the shell." (Eat it). It will never be seen again. (If all the class believes your first statement, then proceed from that thought to show that faith is not seeing but accepting you at your word.)

You see, faith is not seeing but taking God at His Word. In the 11th chapter of Hebrews it says: "Faith is being sure of the things we hope for, being convinced of the things we can't see." (Beck)

None of us was there when God made the world. God's Word tells us that He made it in 6 days by His almighty power. We take God at His word. That is faith.

"By faith we understand that the world was created by the Word of God, so that what is seen was made out of things which do not appear." (Heb. 11:3 RSV)

None of us ever saw Jesus with our physical eyes. We didn't see Him die on the cross on the hill of Calvary. But God's Word tells us that He did die and that He died to take away the world's sins. The apostle Paul states this truth in 1 Corinthians 15:3-4: "I delivered unto you as of first importance what I also received, that Christ died for our sins in accordance with the Scriptures, that He was buried, that He was raised on the third day in accordance with the Scriptures." When we take God at His word and believe that Jesus died "for me," that is faith. Faith is seeing Jesus with spiritual eyes.

None of us has seen heaven. God's Word tells us there is a place called heaven. Jesus said: "In My Father's house are many rooms" (John 14:2). Peter speaks of it as "an inheritance which is imperishable, undefiled, and unfading, kept in heaven for you, who by God's power are guarded through faith for a salvation ready to be revealed in the last time" (1 Peter 1:4-5). We take God at His word and confess, "I believe in the life everlasting." That is faith.

Faith is not something human hearts invent. By nature we are spiritually dead. Faith is worked through God's Word by the power of the Holy Spirit. It is the divinely worked assurance that Christ is our Savior, and that everything God says in His Word is true.

With personal faith in Christ as Savior we learn to look at God's creation through the cross, and the same faith that calls Christ Savior and God Father also acknowledges God as Creator of heaven and earth. This faith looks forward to heaven, accepting as real what is still unseen.

Hebrews 11 is the great faith chapter of the Bible. One of the great heroes of faith listed is Abraham. He took God at His word so implicitly that when God called Him to leave His home and go where God would indicate, he went. "By faith Abraham obeyed when he was called to go out to a place which he was to receive as an inheritance, and he went out, not knowing where he was to go." (Heb. 11:8)

We read of another example of faith in John 4:46-54. A nobleman came to Jesus for help for his sick boy. Jesus said, "Go; your son will live." The nobleman believed the word that Jesus spoke. That was faith.

Let us keep on trusting God's Word in everything. We cannot explain God's creation or the cross or heaven to suit human reason. But faith accepts what is unseen and undemonstrated because God has spoken it. It is taking Him at His word. And why not believe it? "Thy Word is truth," Jesus said (John 17:17). God can be trusted. He doesn't lie.

49. WHAT GOD ORDAINS
IS ALWAYS GOOD

Materials

Paper, pencil, carbon paper, and a large mirror. With the carbon side up under the paper, write in large letters the words: *What God ordains is always good.*

There are many things we wonder about in this life. We have trials, problems, and sickness. Something unexpected sometimes happens, when life is going well. We may get sick or a loved one gets sick. Or perhaps we desire something, and we never seem to get it. We pray and hope, but our prayer does not seem to be answered. Life seems as mixed up and meaningless as the words on this paper. (Display the words.) Who can tell me what they mean? I will give you a secret way to find their meaning. Here is a mirror. This mirror will represent God's revelation of His saving will to us in His Word. (Lay paper flat and angle mirror so that the words will be right side up to the pupils.)

When we take our problems and questions of life to God in prayer, He gives the answer in His Word. What does God say? *"What God Ordains Is Always Good."* He tells us that when we know Him as our Father by faith in Jesus we can trust Him to give us what is needful for this life. His providential will works in harmony with His saving will of grace. "We know that in everything God works for good with those who love Him, who are called according to His purpose." (Rom. 8:28 RSV)

A long time ago there was a woman named Hannah (1 Sam. 1). She and her husband had no children. She wondered why others did and she didn't. Life was so confusing to her. But she went to God with her problem and talked it over with Him. She prayed: "O Lord of hosts, if Thou wilt indeed look on the affliction of Thy maidservant and remember me and not forget Thy maidservant, but wilt give to Thy maidservant a son, then I will give him to the Lord all the days of his life" (1 Samuel 1:11). It was God's will to withhold this blessing from Hannah for a time, and then God granted it to her according to His will and in His own time.

Hannah knew God through His Word as a loving heavenly Father to whom she could talk in prayer. Even if God had not granted her request, the fact that she talked it over with God and saw her problem in the mirror of God's saving will would have enabled her to accept His decision and go on living happily. She prayed aright, adding the condition: "If Thou will indeed look on . . . Thy maidservant."

When we believe "what God ordains is always good," we can talk things over with Him in prayer. If He says yes to our requests, then we will receive them with thanksgiving as Hannah did. If He says, no, or wait, we will accept His will as wiser than our own. We will not grumble and complain against God. Let us see our problems and concerns in the mirror of God's Word as we look with praying eyes of faith.

Joseph in Egypt had this outlook on life too. He said, "As for you, you meant evil against me; but God meant it for good, to bring it about that many people should be kept alive, as they are today" (Gen. 50:20). Joseph knew he could trust the leading of God.

50. WHITE AS SNOW

Materials

A white cardboard heart. A red-orange crayon, red cellophane, a cardboard cross. Make a window in the center of the cross and overlay it with red cellophane. (Use as many thicknesses as necessary to cover the sins on the heart) Check the illustration in connection with the lighting in the room.

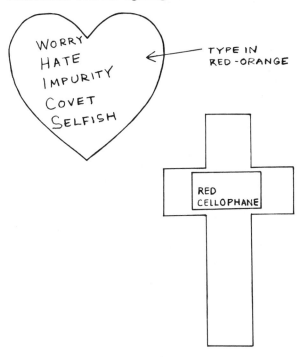

Christians can confess: "I believe in the forgiveness of sins." It is a faith in the forgiving grace of God through Jesus Christ, a trust that He forgives us as often as we need it. (Display white heart.) In our daily walk of life it happens that in a moment of weakness we let hate arise in our hearts against someone. (Write sins on the heart.) We let ourselves be carried away by worry. We let impure thoughts arise. We set our hearts on earthly things and then covet. Often we act selfishly.

Our hearts look like this heart, so full of sins. And we are sorry about them.

God has promised to forgive us for Jesus' sake. Jesus shed His blood on the cross to pay for the guilt and penalty of our sins. This cross with the red window will remind us of God's great gift of His Son to pay for our sins.

When we are sorry that our sins offend God and trust in His forgiveness, it is like bringing this heart under the cross. (Have some pupils look through the red window at the heart.) What do you see? It is white as snow.

Through the prophet Isaiah God asked His people Israel to trust His forgiveness. We read of this in Is. 1:18, where God says: "Come now, let us reason together, says the Lord: though your sins are like scarlet, they shall be as white as snow; though they are red like crimson, they shall become like wool." (RSV)

Scarlet is a color that stays in cloth. Sin is a stain that penetrates the whole human soul with guilt and death. Sin is like scarlet. Only one remedy can take guilt and death away, and that is the blood of Christ. His blood can cleanse each spot because it is the blood of the Son of God.

Many Bible accounts come to mind about forgiveness. Jesus forgave the paralyzed man his sins, saying: "Take heart, My son; your sins are forgiven" (Matt. 9:2).

146

At the first Pentecost Peter said: "Repent and be baptized, every one of you, in the name of Jesus Christ for the forgiveness of your sins" (Acts 2:38). Jesus forgave a sinful woman, saying: "Your sins are forgiven" (Luke 7: 36-50). (See story of Prodigal Son, Luke 15.)

Let us remember that we can come to Jesus just as we are. He alone forgives all.

> Just as I am, without one plea
> But that Thy blood was shed for me
> And that Thou bidd'st me come to Thee,
> O Lamb of God, I come, I come. Amen.

BIBLIOGRAPHY

McLean, W. T. *20 Illustrated Object Lessons*. Grand Rapids: Zondervan Publishing House, 1957.

Ryrie, Charles C. *Easy-to-Get Object Lessons*. Nos. 1,2,3,4. Grand Rapids: Zondervan Publishing House, 1949.

Talbot, Louis T. *Still More Object Lessons That Talk and Teach*. Grand Rapids: Zondervan Publishing House, 1945.

Troke, James Allan, B. D. *Object Teaching Made Easy*. Butler, Ind.: The Higley Press, 1942.

Wilder, Elmer L. *Object Lessons for Boys and Girls*. Grand Rapids: Zondervan Publishing House, 1954.

Index of Scripture Passages

150